FROM ALIGNMENT TO
Enlightenment
THE PATH TO JOY AND PEACE

Gene Black & Edward Muhammad

authorHOUSE®

AuthorHouse™
1663 Liberty Drive
Bloomington, IN 47403
www.authorhouse.com
Phone: 1 (800) 839-8640

Published by AuthorHouse 06/22/2017

ISBN: 978-1-5246-9504-0 (sc)
ISBN: 978-1-5246-9502-6 (hc)
ISBN: 978-1-5246-9503-3 (e)

Library of Congress Control Number: 2017908647

Print information available on the last page.

Introduction

A New Beginning

As children, we are taught about fairy tales and stories that always end happy. Then we grow up in realities that don't support those fairy tales. So, we become jaded, calloused or at the very least we suck it up to say, "this is adulthood...deal." So we do. We "deal." And we live our lives, in silent protest of what does not resemble what was supposed to be our happily-ever-after. We hear the clichés of "Life's a 'b' and then you die." Or "it is what it is." We have all lived this life in some way, shape or form. However, this book, *From Alignment to Enlightenment, The Path to Joy and Peace"* does not subscribe to any of this.

From the very first chapter, *From Alignment to Enlightenment,* begins a journey of breaking down what we have become accustomed to accepting in our lives. The challenges of coping with life's ills and detours. This book is designed to help provide a roadmap to living life joyfully along with an inner peace that is practical and pragmatic in nature. *From Alignment to Enlightenment* is written to propose solutions to everyday problems, issues and challenges while offering activities and exercises that you can apply in your everyday life. This is not "pie-in-the-sky" teaching or a cheerleading session on positive thinking but more so, knowledge and action to be applied immediately to provide you with a stronger hold on creating the sustained happiness you desire.

When we started our blog site, www.aligntoenlighten.wordpress.com back in January 2015, our objective was to share the spiritual empowering knowledge we had gained over the years with as many people as possible. We have seen our fair share of struggle and triumph both personally and professionally. What resounded in us most was the undying spirit of positive anticipation and expectation. We both thought, "positive thinking is wonderful, but how do we make it more actionable? How can we leverage it in our everyday lives?" That's when we started the blog. We wanted to show people how to activate the power that God has given us all. Our passion is to share this knowledge with as many people as humanly possible because it is this same individual power that we all possess as humans that will change our world. Both individually and collectively.

From Alignment to Enlightenment, The Path to Joy and Peace offers you practical application to overcome life's everyday challenges while allowing you to measure those results. The measured results come from how you, as an individual create and manifest the outcomes you desire, and the amount of joy and peace you feel. You will find how powerful the inner you, the ethereal you, the innate you…your soul actually is and how you have the power to manifest any desire. From creating peace within your home and on your job to manifesting the wealth you want; this book has something for everyone. But most importantly, it teaches how to create and sustain love, compassion, peace and tranquility in our lives.

While our blog started off with the sole intent to help others understand spiritual empowerment, we quickly realized that it was us, the authors who were the beneficiaries of the writing we were doing. We both began to experience a deeper calm and feeling of being complete. We both deepened with understanding that authentic joy and peace do not reside in any place outside of ourselves. And when we focus on the people we truly are, we begin to receive what we desire. We have seen the proof of The Law of Attraction, the power of the Universe and have gained an even deeper understanding of our Creator. The most ironic part was while we began to remember our authentic purpose and our individual being, we were compelled to share this same information with as many people as possible. Our lives have been forever changed simply by remembering who we are. As the saying goes, *"we are spiritual beings, having a human experience"*- Pierre Teilhard de Chardin. That understanding allows us to walk in alignment and move toward enlightenment.

As you read *From Alignment to Enlightenment – The Path to Joy and Peace*, you will begin to understand how to manage issues, challenges, opportunities…life in general, in a much more enlightened type of way. Things that used to make your blood boil and your blood pressure rise will now be simple bumps in the road along your life's journey. You will immediately find more joy, peace and tranquility after understanding and applying what you read. Your relationships will strengthen. You will feel more excitement throughout your day. The changes in your life will be immediate and profound. What's more, others around you will see positive change even with the simple aura of more calm surrounding you. More confidence. More peace. More love. More compassion and more understanding. *From Alignment to Enlightenment* is designed to simply and plainly show you the road to sustained joy and peace.

Have you ever thought, "boy, time sure does fly? Seems just like yesterday so-and-so was a baby." Or perhaps we hear a song on the radio and say surprisingly, "that song was from 10 years ago? Wow! Where has the time gone?" We feel this way because we don't live in the moment. We don't spend time in the current space we are in because we are continually looking forward to what we must do next, or backward, regretting what has already transpired. We continually check our smart phones, text messages, emails, etc. Sometimes, it's best to simply slow down…and be present in this moment. Be in the moment to understand how to go *From Alignment to Enlightenment*. What else is more important than understanding what your life on this earth is all about and then living within that purpose to the full extent? What is more important than that?

The first chapter begins your journey to alignment and enlightenment with *Remembering Your Purpose;* a self-exploration of discovery on why you are here. You may not know what your purpose is, but the first chapter points you in the right direction to find out. Begin to understand how your purpose and your perceptions form and shape your life. Continue the discussion and recognize the power of your energy and emotions and how they help to manifest thoughts into things. Turn the corner as we discuss alignment, becoming centered, grounded, calm, peaceful…in command in the midst of any situation. Then conclude with a conversation about enlightenment. Awareness. A new way to see and approach life. And all that this life has to offer. Be aligned. Be enlightened. Be inspired. But most importantly, find the light within yourself and become a beacon unto your own path.

Contents

Purpose and Perceptions

Energy and Emotions

Alignment

Enlightenment

Purpose
and
Perceptions

Purpose and Perceptions

Have you ever thought about or wondered what your true purpose is in life? Have you contemplated the reasons why you are actually here? How about the things you see? Do you readily accept every offer life sends your way as the one true reality you will experience? We are often guided by our perceptions. We are led on a journey of discovery, but we base that discovery on what we have already perceived or what we've already been conditioned to believe and accept as truth. But what is actual truth? And what does truth specifically mean for YOU?

Understanding true purpose and perceptions is about discovering authentic truth within yourself as defined by your soul's purpose in this material world. Explore how your perceptions have shaped the truths and beliefs you have about life. Discovering true purpose inevitably peels back the proverbial onion of life and provides clearer direction for your journey while putting your perceptions into context. In other words, discovering true purpose in life provides clarity of your perceptions and experiences, thus allowing room for your desires to flow and subsequently manifest, which we will discuss in depth in later chapters. But for now, we will focus on your purpose and perceptions.

I recall summertime as a child. No school. Long days. Lots of fun in the neighborhood. I remember my parents would often tell us to be in the house when the streetlights came on. I never understood why because most times we would be right out front with our friends. Nevertheless, we had to be in the house. Two perceptions were happening. As I surmised, my mother's perception was that bad things happen to children outside at night. As for me, I felt

I was being treated unfairly because my friends could be out late and I could not. "For goodness' sakes. Nothing ever happened to THEM when they stayed out and I had to come inside!" is what I would say.

I perceived that there was a lot more fun happening outside while I was forced to come inside. I thought to myself, "One day I'm going to be able to stay out late and have all the fun like everyone else is having." When I turned 13, my mother allowed me to stay out later. This was going to be my coming out party! I was going to have lots of fun after dark like the rest of the kids in the neighborhood because I had perceived and made myself believe this is what was happening. I had given it so much energy to be true that my belief that they were having so much more fun than I was became a truth to me.

So, the day finally came that summer when I was allowed to stay out past dark. My friends and I had been outside for most of the day, riding bikes, going on adventures, playing hide and seek, and so many other fun things kids don't do today. As it got dark, my anticipation grew because I knew it was okay for me to stay out late. The street lights came on and I almost expected the heavens to open and rain down all the fun I had *perceived* I was missing. All I found was more of the same that we had done all day. We talked, laughed, joked…the same as we had done all day long. It was no different. No frills, thrills, or anticipated fireworks. Just hanging out, which was cool! But nothing different happened like I believed. And you know what? I was tired. All in all, it was fun but not what I expected. What I had perceived, what I had made true, and ultimately what I had made my beliefs were NOT the truth at all. There was no additional fun to be had. It was certainly anticlimactic.

Even as grown-ups, the perceptions we count as beliefs or truths in our lives often lead us astray or fool us. We simply accept these falsehoods without challenge. We move, consciously mundane in muted emotion. Our "realities" create our truths instead of our truths creating our realities.

However, when we move along this journey with an understanding of our authentic purpose for being, our authentic truths give birth to our authentic perceptions. Focusing on our true purpose provides clarity regarding our perceptions. When we go within to that peaceful place at the depths of our being, we begin to clear away the cataracts of our consciousness and we find our soul, our factual being, which allows us to see what is real versus what we have perceived to be real. So, "see" from your true and authentic lens. Don't wait for the streetlights to come on to appreciate the fun you experience in the daytime.

Chapter 1

Remembering Your Purpose

Often, I ask my children, "What do you want to do when you grow up?" Having three boys in a 5-year time span, they tend to respond in similar ways that I did when I was their ages; policeman, fireman, basketball star, or like my youngest replied one day, "I'm going to go to work where YOU work." This seems so innocent, which it is at this age and as it should be. But do you find yourself later in life searching for your true purpose? Do you look back on when your parents asked you what you wanted to be when you grew up and do you recall how you responded? Can you look at your current job and say, "YES! I ALWAYS planned on doing this!" Most of us can't say that and it doesn't mean we've made wrong decisions or that we are not happy with what we do. But let's take a journey to truly remembering your purpose for being here.

Let's first establish some truths:

- Regardless of religious preference, we all have a soul, that part of you that exists without tangible proof that you know it exists within yourself. It can be qualified as your conscious, your spirit, your heart. It exists within each of us.
- Your soul is everlasting and eternal. Your soul is ethereal. Your soul communes with God, Allah, Source Power, Jehovah, etc.
- Your soul lived somewhere else (Heaven, paradise, etc.) before you were born to your parents.

- Your body has an expiration date. Your body houses your soul. Your body is perishable while your soul is indestructible on this Earth.
- You chose to come here for a reason. You chose to live in physical form for a time. You chose to come manifest in physical form.

The question to ask yourself is…. why?

Some people's purposes are obvious: Dr. Martin Luther King Jr., Mahatma Gandhi, John F. Kennedy, Michael Jordan, Steven Spielberg, Oprah Winfrey. But what about the everyday man/woman? You CHOSE to come here for a reason. You CHOSE to create, manifest, and construct from the ethereal to the physical. We tend to forget why we came. The imagination of a child is not naïve and uneducated. The imagination of a child is more aligned with the truths of our souls. We grow up and adopt limits on our lives. We should remember the times when there were no limitations on what we could do or create. THIS is our true selves—no boundaries on creation. No limits or glass ceilings. Just a simple understanding that what can be conceived can be created.

Today we almost walk like the horses that pull carriages in cities with the side blinders on as to not be distracted by our surroundings. These side blinders are self-inflicted limits: "I can't pursue my real passion because I have a mortgage." Or "I can't do what I really want because I don't know how I'll get paid." Or "I could NEVER do that because I'm not trained or educated or certified. So I'll just stay where I am and grind it out." Self-inflicted.

Your soul is everlasting, eternal, ethereal, non-perishable, and indestructible in this Earth. You are a powerful being who has been stunted by believing the limitations of your body are also the limitations of your soul. Break free of these thoughts. Who you REALLY are is not the reflection you see in the mirror. Who you REALLY are is the soul that lives within the body. Recognize and understand the power you possess. Remembering your purpose puts you in alignment with who you truly are and why you decided to come here.

So how do you remember your purpose? It's very simple. Ask yourself: What is your passion? What energizes you? What would you do every day of your life even if you didn't get paid to do it? Sing? Write? Dance? Act? Help the homeless? Sweep floors? Clean houses? Save animals? Teach? There are no wrong answers. "But I've got to make a living and I can't follow my passion and make a living!" This is what many people would say. And in doing so, you've just put the horse blinders back on your face.

Invest time in yourself. Take the knowledge you have right now at whatever age you are and go back to when you were 6 years old, free of all boundaries, and ask yourself, "What do I want to do when I grow up?" Discover it all over again. There are no wrong answers. The hardest part of this will be discovering what it is you would do every day without getting paid, discovering your true passion. But it is there. It exists within you and it is asking for you to acknowledge it. You WILL find it. And when you do find it, you'll be more aligned with why you chose to come here. This will be your purpose/s. Now, how do you activate it?

Activate your true passion by focusing on it without limitations, without boundaries, and without restriction. Envision yourself doing that thing you are passionate about. Read about it. Meditate on it. Eat, sleep, drink, and breathe your passion throughout your day, every day. Express your desires about it and, most importantly, allow it to happen. There is no need to "hustle" it or to "muscle" your passion or purpose. Simply express it. Envision it. Expect it.

The Law of Attraction is true. "That which is like unto itself is drawn." In other words, whatever you focus on is attracted to you. The more you envision yourself doing exactly what you chose to come here to do, the more things will come your way that align with that purpose. You don't have to force it into being. It has no choice but to manifest itself. It is the law. Do not get stifled by establishing your own timelines as to when it's supposed to happen for you. God, Source Power, the Universe, Jehovah will continue to pave the road for you in perfect timing. You simply need to know the Law of Attraction is true. "And how will I get paid?" Understand true wealth is living 100% within the reasons you chose to come here. True enlightenment is being aware at all times. Remember your purpose. And find true happiness and wealth by living it.

THINK/WRITE/DO

To begin remembering your purpose in life, try these three simple steps:

1. Identify the top 3 things you love doing. Write them down.
2. Identify the top 3 things you have always admired watching others do. Write them down.
3. Choose one item from both lists and spend 10-20 minutes visualizing and imagining yourself engaging in these activities and earning a living.

When we deliberately set an INTENTION, especially in regard to our purpose, and then activate it by placing our ATTENTION on that thing, we begin to co-create with our Higher Power. We begin to co-create within our authentic purpose for being.

Chapter 2

Escaping the Matrix

"We don't see things as they are. We see them as we are." — *Anais Nin*

One of the first real truths in life is you are a spiritual being. This is your nature. Your intuition, your consciousness, that little voice in your head all allude to the spiritual being of who you are. In the words of renowned author Esther Hicks, *"You are the leading edge of thought."* In other words, your consciousness creates.

To be clearer, the stork didn't bring you. You didn't magically appear, but you chose to come here from the eternity you enjoyed with God, Source Power, Jehovah, Allah, whomever you acknowledge as the all-knowing higher power. You chose to come here to manifest your thoughts and desires into physical things and experiences. That is your fundamental truth.

However, we tend to get caught up in what we call "The Matrix." Yes, very similar to *The Matrix* movie trilogy themes. This "Matrix" keeps us from remembering why we chose to come here and what we chose to come here to do.

If you can remember back to the movie, *The Matrix*, you know all about the surface story—how Artificial Intelligence created a computer construct (The Matrix) of our present day world and, through a hard wire directly into the brain, fed it to humans who were, in reality, kept in incubators and used for their energy output as a power source for the Artificial Intelligence.

In other words, "reality" existed ONLY in the people's minds. It was about how the world relates to the infinite. Everything is one. Everything is connected to everything else and there are subtle ways humans can actually manipulate this reality. The whole 'machine war' in the Matrix movie was just a metaphor of our true reality. The main message then and now is that we have more control of our lives and world, and possess more power than we realize.

Just as in *The Matrix*, reality was understood to be a complex computer simulation created by Artificial Intelligence. Similar to today, we live and experience a world of artificial, superficial, and pseudo intelligence we call technology, all for the purpose of "making our lives a bit more convenient."

Created by a malevolent Artificial Intelligence, the Matrix hid the truth from humanity, allowing people to live a convincing, simulated life while machines grew and harvested people to use as an ongoing energy source. In today's society, we can equate this to the "rat race." While it's silly to think there is some artificial life force directing and creating our every move, we do become callous and our consciousness mutes based on the mundane activities while we do not question our existence. We simply go about life almost in a zombie-like way. We function to satisfy our next desire just to do it all over again tomorrow. This is how we become almost immune to life and authentic reality.

The authentic reality is we are all extensions of infinite intelligence. As the main character in *The Matrix*, Neo, didn't realize his power, so it is with us as we go day to day in a trance-like state, moving almost involuntarily from home to work and back home, with very little if any real purpose in life that we have identified.

As we embark on this journey, let us begin by empowering ourselves to the knowledge of a new reality, a forthcoming of understanding. The clarity of knowing we can have, do, and be anything we choose. We are powerful creators with the ability to bring any desire into being.

Remember the last line in the original Matrix, after Neo has freed the minds of the people and exposed them to the real world, he says, "Where we go next is up to you." Going from Artificial Intelligence to infinite intelligence. Understanding what is authentic versus what is perception, dressed up as truth.

Now you say, "Huh? What are you talking about? I've got bills to pay, a job to do, responsibilities to maintain…this is LIFE!" Yes, it IS life. It is the life you've created from the thoughts you've held and perpetuated as truth and belief. But understand, you are the leading edge of thought. Whatever can be conceived can be created. It is as simple as expressing the desire, holding the vision, and allowing it to happen. As we embark on this journey of aligning your life to enlighten your soul, simply know and understand that the Creator has given you the innate power to accomplish all of the things you want to achieve, create a new reality not only in your mind but in your life, and leverage the real you by unlocking your true purpose. Understand the only things that have stopped or are stopping you from achieving what you desire along the road in THIS life are the speed bumps of doubt, the potholes of worry, and the roadblocks of fear.

Chapter 3

Tell Your Thoughts What to Think

You are the creator of your reality. You are not the orchestrator. That job belongs to God. Your job is to ask and then put yourself in the best position of allowing. Too often we spend time trying to manipulate and control the "how" a thing we want will transpire and we get in the way of what's already being put together. We muddy the waters by our mixed energy. We ask, then through our failed efforts to bring it about, become despondent and doubtful.

Throughout this journey, we will continually stress a few key points:

1. Through alignment, we create our own reality. How? With the help of the Law of Attraction. Like energy attracts like energy.

2. We think thoughts that generate feeling. Those feelings reverberate frequencies/vibrations that translate into physical realities.

Of course, there is a little more to it, which we will discuss in later chapters, but in a nutshell, that's how it works. So if this universal principle is true, and it is true just as much as the Law of Gravity is true, where is the breakdown occurring between what we want and what we have?

"Emancipate yourself from mental slavery. None but ourselves can free our minds." — Marcus Garvey

You must tell your thoughts what to think, tell your feelings what to feel, and tell your body how to respond. Your thoughts will run rampant if you allow them to. You must tell your thoughts exactly what you want them to think. Because we live in a society where we are constantly bombarded with negativity, our minds are filled with images, conversations, and thoughts that are contrary to what we want and desire. If YOU don't tell your mind what to think, who will? If you don't control what you think about, who will? And make no mistake about it—if you don't exercise this control, someone else most certainly will.

Since you get what you think about whether you want it or not, and since whatever your mind is concentrated and focused on, either directly or indirectly, expands, this explains why we stay in a constant, perpetual state of wanting, and not manifesting, or manifesting things unwanted.

When you tell your thoughts what to think, you are simply setting a deliberate intention to reach for the best feeling/thought you can, at any given time. The operative word here is *deliberate*. Change perspective by thinking on purpose, speaking on purpose, and thus acting with purposeful intention. Be as picky, if not more, about the thoughts you think as you are about the healthy or non-healthy foods you choose to eat. We have all experienced what happens to our bodies when we repeatedly make poor nutrition choices. Things can be just as, if not more detrimental when we make poor thought choices.

Why is this important?

If you can control your thoughts by instructing what you want them to be, you will then also be able to guide and direct your emotions, feelings, and mood. The two go hand and hand. Reaching for good feeling/thoughts produces good feelings/emotions. This in turn produces the manifestation of things you desire. Once thought and emotions are intentionally directed towards that which feels good and right, you then have options as to how you want to respond to any given circumstance or situation. So instead of knee-jerk reacting to someone cutting you off in traffic, decide on the emotion you truly desire and act on that. You are now in the driver's seat instead of being driven. You are now no longer guided by the things you see, hear, smell, touch, and taste; things which often lead us astray. But rather now you are guiding and shaping YOUR LIFE how YOU wish for it to be. You are now a co-creator with God creating how your life will turn out.

And here is the point where the manifestation of your true wants and desires lies. Here is where the Universe responds favorably to your request through the frequency you are emitting. There is no muddy water. Your intentions are clear and focused. It's like God is saying, "Okay, looks like he/she is clear on their desires now. We can give them what they want." And remember—**you can never outpace your readiness for what you want.** When you are truly ready for something, it will manifest, granted you've made your request known with clear and deliberate intentions while believing and envisioning yourself in it. Things will begin to take place that you cannot, and could not have even perceived. Our job is not to perceive how. **Our job is to simply conceive and believe**. You conceive, believe, and receive. God, through universal laws and spiritual principles, does the rest. God exercises power through YOU! God is Creator and we are extensions of that Source. Since we are created in the image of God, we are co-creators with the ability to exercise the power of creation in our lives.

Once you realize this, you can choose how you wish to live, recognizing that there is a choice and you can emancipate yourself from simply living a reactionary life. A life of observe-respond-observe-respond is not living. Especially when you can exercise greater control and dominion, and produce the life you want and would rather have, a life of experiences that you have deliberately created.

At first it will seem somewhat difficult if you have not been accustomed to living your life in this way. But once you get the hang of it, it will become natural and actually fun. You will feel empowered that you can control your own thoughts. When things begin to manifest for you EXACTLY the way you intended, you will feel a tremendous sense of mastery!

> *"If this time/space reality has the ability to conceive and inspire a desire within you, then this same time/space reality has the ability to manifest the means to fulfill that desire." — Esther Hicks.*

THE HOW IS NOT YOUR BUSINESS! God is the orchestrator. God is the one moving things around, manipulating, causing all circumstances, events, and people to coincide in perfect harmony to bring about just what you've asked for. But you must remain steadfast on the desire and not allow doubt, fear, impatience, or any other negative emotion to creep in and become the dominant emotion along your journey. This is where you tell your thoughts what to think and remind yourself—"I am a creator. I am a deliberate creator and my life is being tended to from behind the scenes."

Chapter 4

Circumstances Don't MATTER

How often do you feel unhappy because of the circumstances you experience? Would you like to be able to feel happy whatever happens around you? Do you believe that this is even possible? So often we let our circumstances influence the way we feel. The lack of money, problems at work, quarrels with a partner, with family or with friends; all can contribute to a feeling of unhappiness if we allow it. We begin to believe this is the natural way. Remember: YOU CREATE YOUR OWN REALITY and therefore can change the way you experience life.

It is not our circumstances that matter. **It's only your state of being that MATTERS—or, better yet, only your state of being materializes (becomes matter).** Only state of being or consciousness can create matter/physical reality.

Matter is subject to consciousness. Consciousness is not subject to matter. This is how we turn thoughts into things. Literally. This is how we apply the notion of "be and it is." Turning the non-physical reality into the physical reality is more about inside/internal work than about outside, physical action. Not that the action-oriented approach to manifestation is not needed. There are definitely physical things that we must do, deadlines to meet, goals to achieve, etc. However, if you believe and understand that we are mostly non-physical beings/energy/vibration, then it stands to reason that most of the work is with the non-physical aspect of ourselves. Therefore "circumstances don't matter."

It's our state of being, mindset, mood, etc. that translates into physical manifestations. This is literally how our thoughts manifest into things. But for most, it's the other way around. We usually let our life experiences and circumstances dictate our state of being, which keeps us in a perpetual state of responding to every life event that comes up. When things are going well, we feel well. If things are going badly, we feel badly. Usually we give our greatest attention and focus to the "bad" or unwanted things instead of the wanted or "good" that we experience. Someone asks us how we're doing, and we make statements like, "I'm hanging in there" or "I'm making it." These responses are mostly based on how things are going in our lives right at that moment. What's your perspective of life? What is your usual response when you're greeted by someone? Of course this is an easier concept spoken than practiced. But it is certainly worth auditing our expectations and evaluating our desires. As Emily Dickinson wrote, *"Dwell in the possibility."* Align your mind state with your expectations and desires. Live in THAT space.

We experience "bad news" and "good news" and we tend to respond according to our interpretation of that information. Situations and events are nothing more than circumstances, devoid of any meaning besides what we give it. Only our interpretations and judgment of them give the things we experience meaning. Our true experience of reality is only reflective of our interpretations of it. We should better understand the duality of things.

There is always the yin and the yang, the "good" AND the "bad." There is no intrinsic meaning or value to anything. So our view of things is simply a point of view, a conscious and deliberate choice made at any given moment to experience the things we experience. So it stands to reason that we can choose to change our life experience by changing our point of view…changing our state of being. This resets our point of attraction, which the Universe is constantly responding to. By changing your focus to your expectations and your desires, you are emitting a much stronger vibration to what you want to attract. When something undesirable or "bad" is happening and we focus our energies on the "bad" in the situation, we emit the vibration that aligns with the "bad."

Conversely, the opposite happens when we focus our attention on the "good." Therefore, when the "bad" things are happening, it is imperative for us to change our focus to impede the "bad." We do this by directing the focus of our desire and expectation.

If your circumstances are telling you that you don't have enough money, change your focus to first identifying and FOCUSING on what you are grateful for that your current finances CAN afford. Put mental power to it. Then start to envision yourself with more than enough money. Finally, focus on how you will spend that money when you receive it. This does not mean that all of a sudden you'll receive a boatload of wealth (although you might), but simply watch, pay attention and acknowledge when and how things begin to work in your favor financially because you have changed your focus from "being broke" to being wealthy.

I once knew a gentleman who, without fail, would respond "I'm perfect" every time I'd ask him how he was doing. At the time, I didn't know what to make of his response. Was he being facetious or sarcastic? Was he trying to portray himself outwardly in some "I've always got myself together" type of way? This was his response to me and others for the 10-15 years I came in contact with him. The man has since passed away and I never asked him about his responses. But I do understand now why or, better yet, how he responded as such.

"I'm perfect" does not mean everything in your life is going exactly the way you want it to. But, rather, you've found a level of appreciation and gratefulness for precisely where you are. It's understanding that the circumstances you encounter, no matter how dire they may appear at the time, don't have any real power over you unless you allow them too. The Universe will respond in kind to whatever you feel. Therefore, only project what you want to receive in return. Choose to be healthy. Choose to be wealthy. Choose to be happy. Choose to be powerful. Choose to be joyous. When we begin to practice controlling the way we feel, controlling the mood we allow ourselves to be in, only then can we begin to turn thoughts into things, manifesting those things we really want in life, and accept life's circumstance just as they are—circumstances.

THINK/WRITE/DO

- When you wake up tomorrow morning, before you get out of bed, choose what type of day you will have. Contemplate what you have chosen throughout the day. Pay attention to all opportunities, because they will come, that you encounter that support what you chose before you got out of bed. For example, if you chose to have a happy and joyous day, don't ignore the stranger who speaks to you and greets you with a warm smile on the street. Reciprocate the feeling. When we do, those positive energies continue to expand.
- As circumstances occur, whether they are small or large, practice seeing yourself on the other side of the circumstance. Say these words: "This situation has no real power over my day. I choose at this moment to feel empowered, positive, and determined to see the very best in this situation. This circumstance does not matter. Only my state of being matters."
- At the end of your day, take 10 minutes to think about what you chose in the morning and compare that to how your day turned out.

This will be a process. But when you practice choosing your emotion, you will, more times than not, receive what you chose. You are a powerful creator in this space. When you desire it, focus on it and expect it, whatever you've chosen will show up. Remember, *"Dwell in the possibility"*

Chapter 5

Your Five Senses Don't Tell You the Whole Truth

We are all acutely aware of our 5 senses: Touch, Smell, Taste, Hearing, Sight. We tend to think we are complete if we have access to all five of our senses. They help us shape our views of the world. *Touch* is important to give us perspective regarding the objects around us. It also helps keep us safe from things that are too hot or cold. Or we use it as a form of affection and reassurance. *Smell* activates various sensations and even emotions in our brains, from the smell of beautiful flowers, to sparking feelings of nostalgia during Thanksgiving at Mom's house. *Taste* is essential for the things we ingest, yet we struggle with the "good tasting" things as they seem to be the same things that cause us to gain weight! *Hearing* also is vital as we employ this sense when determining meaning through words, tone, and inflection. *Sight* provides us the view of our world and we make important decisions based on what we see. We may choose a home, a car, our clothes, or even a mate based on what we see. All in all, we depend on our five senses to help determine our every move in life. And isn't it interesting when we see those people who may be missing one or more of their five senses so another one or more of the senses pick up the slack. The person may have a heightened sense of hearing if their eyesight is impaired. Or they may have a better sense of smell if they've lost their hearing. The Creator has made us perfect in this way, allowing us to leverage our senses to interpret the world we live in. So, in all of God's perfectness, why are our senses leading us astray?

Let's first revisit a couple of fundamental truths: God is all powerful. We come from an ethereal place or, better said, a place of non-material. We are ethereal beings, which is why we have a soul. Our souls are our true selves, the evidence being that our bodies perish every day, but our souls are everlasting. We were made in the image of the Creator. Therefore, we too have the ability to create in this physical/material world.

How do we determine value in the material world? Why do we value diamonds? Who said $100 is worth what it can purchase? What makes an exotic sports car so valuable? When was it decided that the cost of land in Southern California was worth more than the same property in Southern Florida? Don't be alarmed. I understand economics, free trade, and financial valuation. The point is, WE have given these things meaning. WE have given these things value. WE have given these things power in our lives and associated them with being "comfortable" to appease our five senses. And, at the same time, we have become slaves to THINGS to help determine our happiness, prestige, social status, and mental comfort. The fact is, diamonds are simply five carbon atoms fused together. Dollars are made of 75% cotton and 25% linen fibers. Exotic sports cars are faster than average, but you can't drive them to their potential without running the risk of being imprisoned. The weather in Southern California is very similar to Southern Florida, minus the humidity. We are being defined by the material things we have created or given value to. We sometimes allow material things to define who we are in this physical world. We have become dependent upon our five senses to define our lives and give meaning to who we are. It is at this stage where we have lost all creative power God has empowered us with.

There was a news article that spoke about a new breakthrough in military intelligence. The government and military developed an "invisible suit" that will eventually aid soldiers in combat. I can't tell you all about the technical aspects of it, but, in short, the suit, when worn by a soldier, would bend light. When light is bent at the right vector, a physical object can become non-visible to the human eye. This is a great example of the limitations of our senses. Some time ago there was a big social media sensation about the infamous "dress." Is it blue and black or white and gold? As a people, we are entirely too invested and solely reliant on our senses. We completely neglect the innate power of creation God has given us and now rely on what has already been created by man. We trust it completely. This is why our senses have led us astray.

"What's beyond five senses?" **Awareness**. Become aware. Strive to become fully aware. "What does that mean?" It means KNOW who and what you really are.

"How do you find that out?" A great place to start is through meditation. Reach the place of void in your mind so you may commune with your true self. While in a meditative state, one goes beyond the reliance of the five senses and embarks on a higher plane that operates outside of them.

> *"For if you empty the brain of all thoughts (as in a state of meditation), awareness turns out not to be empty, void and passive. Beyond the limits of time and space, one process—and only one—is taking place. Creation is creating itself, using consciousness as its modeling clay. Consciousness turns into things in the objective world, into experiences in the subjective world." — Deepak Chopra, The Book of Secrets*

Understanding and adopting these principles allow us to touch on the reasons why we exist while empowering and activating our God-given creative powers. Your five senses put limitations on what is possible and are governed by this physical world. The five senses are given to help protect the body and allow your body to experience all life has to offer. Your consciousness and awareness are given to help create and deliver your desires and purpose within this physical world.

People often say, "Perception is reality." Well, that's true if you are solely reliant on your five senses. But the real fact is, we create the perception and then become the star of our own "reality show." Your senses should not create your primary reality. Your primary reality is created by your consciousness and awareness. Create the life you desire by spending time with your true self in a meditative state. While this may seem foreign to some, this is all natural and innate to your being. What can be conceived, can be created. This is the natural order of things.

Billions of cells within your body have been destroyed and created in the time it has taken you to read these chapters. They serve a purpose with the natural order of things. By becoming aware and leveraging your consciousness and creative prowess within a meditative state, you have the ability to create and manifest your desires within this physical world. This too is the natural order of things. Try not to limit your abilities based on what you can see, feel, taste, touch, and/or hear. Unleash your true ability by becoming aware of the innate creative power God has already granted to make clear and apparent desired outcomes and physical things. In short, rather than being enslaved by your five senses, be emancipated by your consciousness.

THINK/WRITE/DO

Reaching the ethereal you…the authentic you…becoming fully aware can begin with meditation. Meditation helps us touch on that part of ourselves, our soul, that is the direct connection with our Creator. It is this space where the five senses end and our consciousness begins.

Here are a few steps to get you started if meditation is new to you or if you'd like a good exercise to become more aware. This is a simple relaxation exercise to help put you in a meditative state. The more you do this, the longer you will be able to go and the deeper you will go into meditation.

- Find someplace quiet and plan on being uninterrupted for at least 15 minutes.
- Sit with good posture, arms and hands relaxed, and feet flat on the ground. (This is an important part of grounding yourself, literally.)
- Close your eyes and begin to take notice of your breathing. Breath normally. Just become aware of the fact you are breathing and focus on it.
- Now, imagine there is a big bucket of goo (yes, goo) resting on a shelf above your head. The goo won't hurt you. In fact, the goo is designed to magically relax any part of your body it touches.
- Imagine the goo starts to pour over the top of your head. It's totally okay because you can still breathe just fine. Let the goo

pour down slowly over the top of your head, down your face, over your shoulders.

- Continue to focus on your deliberate breathing while the goo flows down your chest, your back, your thighs, legs, calves, feet, and toes.
- Let the goo flow very slowly. Imagine the goo flowing slowly. Every place the goo touches relaxes that part of your body. Just relax… and breathe.
- By the time the goo has reached the soles of your feet, you should be extremely relaxed. Don't think. Simply continue to be relaxed while focusing on your breathing.

It is in this place of silence and relaxation where we find the peace and tranquility of our souls. This is where we locate our consciousness and awareness. Consider doing this for three days a week. You will find that same peace and tranquility will begin to carry over into your everyday life. Why? Because now you've touched on the true essence of who you are.

Chapter 6

Protect Your Perceptions

We've talked about creating your own reality. We've talked about escaping the "matrix" to live in your true purpose. We've spoken about many things that have to do with what you perceive, create, and manifest from within. In short, we've spoken a lot from an inward/outward perspective. At the end of the day, we create our very own realities. Every human being's "reality" is unique to them. Why? How is that so? Because we all experience life in an individual manner that is unique to us. No two people experience life in the exact same way. Therefore, how we define our realities is unique to our own experiences.

We live in this world of individually created realities. We share in those realities with others and we collectively form beliefs when we collectively agree on any given perception. In the previous chapter, we talked about your five senses and how they can be deceiving or not show you the entire picture of what true reality is. In the midst of this controlled chaos, one must be very careful with what is perceived in all areas. Protect your perceptions. Perceptions are not just what you see but also what you hear, taste, smell, and touch.

How do perceptions affect our emotions? A few examples. The musical artist Pharrell produced and sang a popular song, "Happy." Taking a broad stroke, I'd say that for many people, the song innately creates a sense of exhilaration and excitement. It lifts the spirit and makes you want to dance. Hearing. Another example is in regards to a poll of 100 women where 65% responded that eating chocolate provides similar comfort and similar feelings of satisfaction as having sex. Taste. Have you ever noticed the feeling of calm and serenity you feel when watching the sunset? Seeing. I met a car dealer one time who told me that instead of pumping loud, boisterous music, he plays classical melodies and puts jasmine in the air vents. The purpose was to make customers feel relaxed. Smell. Have you ever gotten a massage from a good-looking person versus one that was less attractive? How did you perceive that? Did you notice the difference even though they were both professional? Touch. Perceptions are created from the things we hear, taste, see, smell, and touch. Perceptions influence and direct thought as well as emotion.

Conversely, do you feel like cuddling with your loved one after listening to pounding heavy metal rock? Probably not. Do you feel a sense of comfort from the taste of medication? No. Do you get overjoyed by watching a car crash? I doubt it. Do you feel relaxed and at ease when you smell hot garbage? Unlikely. Do you feel comforted when some stranger touches you? Doubtful. What's the point? Your perceptions are created from the things you hear, taste, see, smell, and touch. Perceptions help shape our beliefs and thus our reality by influencing and directing thought and emotion.

Understanding how we feel and the things that surround us to make us feel a certain way is vitally important to our well-being. But we tend to live the life of a soap opera. It's "The Reckless & Ridiculous." How many more times do you need to see somebody fighting on a Facebook video? There are videos of people being stabbed, shot, and killed all over the Internet and then reposted for others to see. Why has the *Jerry Springer* show been on for so long? Over 25 years of "surprises" and fist fights. In a world of highly contested ratings, a show can only remain if the public demands it. Why do we sit on the edge of our seat wondering "who the daddy is" on the *Maury Povich Show*? Then we revel in the joy and the impending berating the man gives the woman when Maury says, "You are NOT the father!" (And the crowd goes wild while the woman collapses in tears.) And by far, the most incredibly ironic debacle of them all….how many more "reality" shows can be made and become popular? It seems we have become a society calloused and infatuated with what we perceive as shock and awe. Watching others sling mud from afar seems to be the draw. It's watching a train wreck in slow motion and we can't seem to turn away from the impending disaster of someone else's life. And it's "okay" as long as it's not happening to us. But the real facts are we are affected by what we perceive and how we distinguish, classify, and interpret what we perceive. There is no escaping that. Even when you THINK you are not affected, subconsciously, you are.

I remember being in 3rd grade, learning about fruits and vegetables, and my health teacher saying, "You are what you eat." I didn't understand that when I was a child. But now I understand that the foods I intake become a part of who and what I am. My body and mind are directly affected by the food I ingest. Therefore, 'you are what you eat.' By that same token, your inner being is directly affected by what you intake. Positivity begets positivity. Negativity begets negativity. The Law of Attraction is absolute. If we find pleasure and enjoyment at the destruction of others, it becomes a part of our inner being and begins to perpetuate itself in our lives. That same negativity begins to manifest itself in other areas where you least expect it.

The same holds true for when we surround ourselves with what we consider positive energy. Positivity begins to manifest itself in other areas of life where you least expect it. It is Universal Law. This is why certain songs you hear, certain things you taste, different smells, touches, and definitely things you see, affect your emotions. Your inner being perceives those things as positive or negative and processes them as such. They become a part of YOU.

So, to that end, be a fierce, relentless protector of your perceptions so you may truly perceive what is authentic and right for YOUR life. If not, your perceptions will create your reality for you. It's not that fighting on Facebook or watching the *Jerry Springer* show or reality television is "wrong." This is not about what we consider to be right or wrong. This is about YOU and what YOU desire and what YOU want to attract into your life.

Let's talk about beauty for example. Beauty is individually defined but has been qualified, compartmentalized, and socialized by societal measurements of body types, body weights, skin tones, and a host of other physical attributes. But think about the authentically beautiful people who resonate with you. It goes beyond their physical appearance. There is something about their spirit that qualifies them as beautiful to you. Think about comparing the beauty of a manufactured sports car to the beauty of a meadow rich with flowers in full bloom. Authentic beauty sparks an emotion from deep within. It is attractive to our souls not just to our eyes. We are drawn to it. It is positivity that compounds upon itself. Therefore, if you desire to be beautiful, then surround yourself with authentically beautiful people, things, and places that appeal to the eyes of your soul. Take time to be quiet and alone with yourself, which will attract serenity, peace, and calm. Enjoy the silence. Watch awe-inspiring things that inspire and align with what is truly awesome to YOU instead of awe-shocking things that create callous consciousness. Keep a song in your heart. Stop and smell the roses—*literally.* Reinforce compassion and empathy with your loved ones through encouraging words instead of criticism. Underline your adoration with the reinforcement of a gentle touch.

Protecting your perceptions protects your inner being. Protecting your inner being clears the way for your consciousness and allows it to grow. Allowing your consciousness to grow provides a way for you to be full and complete at any level of life you choose. Including the current level where you are. Be protecting of yourself. Care for yourself. Love…yourself.

THINK/WRITE/DO

As we mentioned in this chapter, we should be protective of those things we expose our 5 senses to. By proactively surrounding ourselves with things that support that effort, we subtly remind our consciousness what is real with our souls. Try the following:

- **Hear**—Every morning and/or throughout your day, choose a song, old or new, that makes you feel uplifted, joyous, and exalted. Be in the moment with the song you're listening to. Is it the lyrics, the music, the melody that make you feel good? Focus on whatever makes you feel happy with that song and listen to it daily.

- **Taste**—Choose to eat or drink something that you truly enjoy every day. If that something you enjoy so much is going to add another million calories to your diet, don't do that! But certainly, find something that you can enjoy every day that you look forward to savoring. Or a meal you can look forward to, e.g., having coffee in the morning and taking the time to savor it, going to your favorite place for lunch with a friend, etc. Remember to be in that moment.

- **Sight**—There is so much beauty that surrounds us daily. Take some time to simply admire the trees outside, the birds in the air, or the crisp breeze on an early autumn day. Look at that picture of your kids on your desk that has been sitting there for years. Buy yourself a bouquet of flowers. Surround yourself with beautiful things man cannot create.

- **Smell**—Have you ever smelled a baby? Babies smell like heaven (most times). If there's no baby readily available, take the time to enjoy the way you smell after you've just showered, or after you've washed your hair. Stop to smell the roses you just bought yourself to support your sight. Go outside and take a deep breath of fresh air just because. Whatever is pleasing to your nose, take the time to smell it. Daily.

- **Touch**—Touch doesn't always have to be with another human, although we highly recommend finding comfort in a loved one's touch daily because it is an awesome way to support and protect your perceptions. But if no one is available, keep something close that makes you feel comfort when you touch it. That could be a blanket, a pet, a sweater, etc. Whatever makes you feel calm and comfortable when you touch it, do that.

Protecting your perceptions is not only a defensive exercise. It is an offensive exercise where you have the power to control and, more importantly, manage what you perceive.

Chapter 7

Stop 'Telling It Like It Is' and Tell a New Story

For many of us, our lives up to this point have reflected the stories we've told and have been told while our future life will be the stories we keep telling ourselves and others right now. One of the best ways to change your life is to tell a new story of who you want to be and how you want your life to be. Live your vision.

Too often the stories we tell address the "right now" issues that are happening in our lives. We say things like, "Life is hard. There aren't enough hours in the day." Or "I wish I were more organized, had more money, had a better life, etc."

Someone asks how you're doing, how's it going, and we say, "Oh, I'm okay, could be better," or "I could complain but I won't," or "I'm alright I guess." The tendency is to address the NOW way you feel or the NOW way things are transpiring in your life. So, if it's going well, we tell stories of how well things are going, or if it's not going so well, we tell stories of that. And isn't it interesting that even when things are going well we often have a fear of impending doom lurking around the corner, or some catastrophic event that's about to happen and wipe away our feel-good moment. It's never long that we bask and relish in the moment of all being well before we, through our thoughts, create a different reality of drama, despair, and turmoil of some kind. We've been conditioned as a society to expect the worse and hope for the best. A more authentic way to adjust our expectations is to expect the best. Period. Expect the best possible outcomes to any and everything we experience.

Have you ever noticed that some of the best speakers in the world tell great stories? Many successful public speakers and lecturers know the art and science to storytelling and the power it generates in delivering a point or concept. Have you also noticed the times when you connected with a speaker and really felt the message he/she was attempting to deliver was through a story? How does this work and why should we use this tool for creating better lives for ourselves? What does the art of storytelling do to the teller and the listener?

The Universe, like the subconscious mind of man, does not know the difference between fact and fiction. It does not know if the vibration you are offering is because of what you are imagining or truly experiencing. In either case, it is responding. The Universe functions off the emotional vibration you are offering. What do stories do? They tap into the emotion of not only the listener but certainly the teller.

Have you ever been telling a story of something that happened in your life and felt yourself becoming very emotional in the telling of the story— high levels of excitement, anger, happiness, disgust, joy, etc.? Sure, we've all experienced this. The emotion of our real-life story is authentic. You feel a certain way when telling the story. Leveraging your imagination or your desired outcomes is one way to help manifest your authentic desires.

When you envision where you want to be in life, whether that is regarding your personal attributes or material things, develop the story you want to tell. It is at this point where the imagination acts and the Law of Attraction begins orchestrating your life based on YOUR STORY. Now, this does not mean that exact prototypes and details of your story will be reflected (although oftentimes it does happen exactly like that). What it means is that the essence of the way you feel in telling your story reflects back to you and the Universe works to provide you with life experience that is based on the dominant emotional vibration you are offering. This is why it is vitally important to start telling your life story the way you want it to be. NOT the way that "it is" or the way you perceive it.

We often brag about keeping it "real" and "I'm just telling it like it is." Well, now we know, telling it like it is only gets you more of what that is.

If you want something different, you have to talk less about what it is and more about what is coming.

Every time you tell your new story, your belief in the new story becomes stronger. This is how people lie about something repeatedly and it becomes their truth. They believe the untruth and their minds have come to accept what once was untrue as now true. Every time you tell the new story, your belief in the new story becomes stronger. Your imagination automatically starts creating a clearer picture of the desired end result, as well as images of you in the process of living the new story. Every time you tell the new story, you're feeling better about yourself and life in general. All this combined creates your vibration of attraction and how you vibrate (feel) is how you attract everything into your life.

Consider yourself a movie director or play writer. Your life is the storyline and you have complete creative control. What would the next scene be? The next chapter? How do the characters in your story interact with you? Who are the supporting characters? Because that's what every person in your life is—supporting cast members in your very own "movie." And, most importantly, how does your story end? If your life/movie isn't what you want it to be, WRITE A NEW AND DIFFERENT STORY!

Tell the "My Life Is Really Wonderful" story. Tell the "I'm Blessed and Fortunate" story; the "Life Is Really Good" story. Tell the story of abundance and prosperity; the Isn't Life So Good to Me? story. And then watch how the Universe yields evidence and facts to support your new story. Some would say, "But if I say these things and it's not true, I'm lying to myself." And there is merit to this point; however, it is your belief about a particular thing along with your expectation through which change occurs. Therefore, create what is true for YOU.

If you're trying to 'fake it 'til you make it,' but do not believe the new story you are telling yourself, you will have a harder go at making life changes. However, there are ways to bridge the gap and empower your belief about your story.

Simple word play will make a huge difference. For example, "I am beginning to feel better. I am beginning to like the way my life is going. I am becoming exactly the person I want to be. I like the way my life is beginning to unfold. Things are becoming easier for me to achieve. Money, prosperity, and abundance are becoming clearer in my life experience." Using different words softens the story and provides some ease to believing the story you are telling. Of course, this takes practice and consistency, but with just a little motion in this direction you will feel a difference.

Remember… you are the creator of your own movie, and everything is all about your personal perception and how you like it. You get to choose exactly how you want things to be. You get to create the plot, the scene, and conclusion exactly the way you want it to be. Whether it be fiction or fact as you currently see it, the more you write and recite the new story, the more it manifests into fact for your life experience. It is law. And the fact of the matter is you're already doing this anyway without realizing it. By default, you have created your life as it is. The life you currently live is a culmination of the stories you've told yourself either silently or repeated aloud. So why not be deliberate with the things you want in your life? Try it. When you start telling your new story, you are thinking new thoughts and creating a new vibration. Because of this, you will receive impulses and hunches from your inner guidance to take action towards living the new story. **Be sure to take the action and follow the impulses that feel good and right for you.** Why not be intentional with your desires and be the true creator you were born to be? You have nothing to lose and everything to gain. Write your new story today!

THINK/WRITE/DO

- **Identify Your Story**—The first step in changing a limiting belief is identifying it.

  Think about the various things you may be discontented with in your life. Don't be shy. Write them out on paper. "Tell it like it is." Or perhaps at least the way you see it right now.

- **Shift Your Story**—Now that you've identified your story, you should create a new one for yourself.

  Take each statement and create a new story. For example, you may have written, "I don't have any money." A new story would be, "My life is filled with abundance." You may have written, "I need to lose weight." A new story would be, "I'm on the road to living the healthiest life I can live." Whatever the statement of discontent you've written, write a new story, which will offer a vibration that coincides with your true desires.

- **Emotions Are Key**

  Put this paper in a place where you will have access to reading it frequently and do just that—read it frequently. But don't just recite the words. Feel it emotionally. The more you feel what you're saying, the stronger the vibration you offer. The stronger the vibration you offer, the quicker you begin to manifest what you desire.

- **Nothing happens Without (Inspired) Action**

  Now that you have a new story about your life, you'll be able to see opportunities in places you've never noticed them before. You will also now have the courage to try things you once may have been afraid to try.

Pay close attention to the signs and signals that appear to you after having created your new story. The signs may or may not be obvious, but they most definitely will appear. When they do, ACT ON THEM! Do whatever inspires you the most at that time keeping in mind the new story you've created. Do this over and over again until you see the manifestation of your new story unfolding before your very eyes.

Chapter 8

Lose Your Luggage

Chances are, if you've flown on airplanes enough, you may have had an experience where the airline lost your luggage. This usually involves some type of frustration, anger, angst, and inconvenience. It especially leaves you in the lurch if you have immediate plans and you need the clothes you so meticulously planned and folded properly.

So, when we say, "Lose Your Luggage," we certainly are not speaking about your packed clothing. (Although, this WOULD give you a good reason to go shopping for a new wardrobe.) But in this context, losing your luggage refers to losing the luggage of your past. The complete 14-piece set, including the carry-on bag packed to the brim with bricks of regret, mitigating stories, and judgment against yourself and others. This luggage only serves to weigh you down along your journey in life.

Why is it that we continue to lug around feelings, emotions, and experiences from the past? Why is it that we allow the past to dictate our circumstances of the present? Why do we use the past to measure our current moments? Why do we depend on the past to define our present day? If you don't have a good answer to any of the questions, it should be a good indicator that it's time to lose your luggage. But instead, we tend to fold up our self-imposed judgments, put our past relationships on hangers, and we carefully pack away our worries, past troubles, and fears into our suitcase of life and carry them around like prized possessions, ready to pull them back out and put them on display whenever a current situation arises. Understand that the past has no power. The past has no power of judgment or measurement, nor is it an indicator of your future.

Any given moment, **if you are cognizant of the moment you're currently in**, allows you to create a brand-new moment that alters the course you want to be on. But we tend to allow our luggage to dictate which trip we will take. Will we go on a "guilt trip" today? Leveeing guilt against ourselves and handing out guilt to others? Will we ride the "Angry Train" and hold onto how you felt back in 1989 because you haven't reached the destination the "Angry Train" is taking you to? You haven't let it go therefore you're still riding it out. Or perhaps you want to jump on the "Poor Me Plane" and fly to a destination of never being good enough or placing the blame on others for why things happen the way they do in your life.

Again, ask yourself a question here and try to provide a good answer: At what point in time would you pack your bags, head to the airport and allow your bags to dictate where you are traveling to? This would be ridiculous, right? Then it is just as ridiculous to allow your emotional baggage or your luggage of previous circumstances and choices to dictate your current moment. There is no such thing as controlling the past or even controlling the future. The **only** reality is in the present. The **only** control is how you decide to feel in this moment. If you don't like how you feel within any given moment, then change the destination and set out on a new course.

To be clear, there is no real *road* to enlightenment. Enlightenment is not a destination but simply a state of being. It simply is. However, for the sake of making a point, in this context, we will refer to enlightenment as a road. So, as we travel down this road, with enlightenment being our destination, the first articles we must release to lighten our luggage load is self-imposed judgment.

Stop holding onto things of the past you consider "mistakes." We all make choices along the road and those choices alter our directions in life. It doesn't make them good or bad. They simply are. If you made a choice and it didn't align with your desired outcome, it's simply what happened.

It doesn't make it a good or bad decision. When you take time to dwell on and accept that point, you will immediately feel lighter and more free. You will have lightened your load for easier travel on your trip. Release the judgment of your choices and simply be guided by your current moment and what you desire. Holding onto judgment of yourself is like packing bricks in your suitcase and carrying them around.

Next, lose judgment of others. How many times have you considered a relationship with someone else and said, "Yeah, but he/she has too much baggage." What baggage is it that they have? Emotional baggage? Children outside of you? A "bad" history of breakups or cheating? Does that become the barometer or measuring stick of how you will be treated in the relationship? We unequivocally answer, "YES!" immediately passing judgment on the actions of another's past to dictate our future. It is in THIS moment we stall out the journey of experience. But ask yourself again, "What is it that I desire in the current moment?"

We say, "Well, based on past experience, I know if X does this then Y is going to happen." In that moment, we have made decisions based on the past that are predicting our future. Again, these are two things we have zero control over! The past and the future. What we have is the moment. This is not to say that a man who has a history of domestic abuse should be welcomed into a woman's life without expecting he will abuse her. But understanding the NOW and being present and aware within the NOW is what provides the fertile ground for your desires to grow.

Begin by expressing your desires to God, Jehovah, The Creator, The Universe, Allah. Only seek to control what you **feel** in that moment and every moment going forward. Focus those feelings and live in a state of love and gratitude. Watch your desires unfold before you in every created moment. When living in a constant state of awareness, the only true reality is the current moment you are experiencing. The current moment you are experiencing is where creation is born. It is the only thing you control. Therefore, carrying the baggage of your past experiences or the baggage of others' past circumstances holds zero power except for the power you give it. It does not dictate the future and is not an overall indicator of outcomes.

As you strike out on your journey, become aware of your current moment and relinquish the past. The past has already left you. So why continue to court it? Leave it and create a new moment. Whatever type of moment you want to create. Stop lugging around self-doubt, anxiety, fear, and false expectations based on past and previous experiences and choices. This is dead weight. In every literal sense of the meaning, the past is dead and it is unnecessary weight. Lighten the load of your journey by losing your luggage.

THINK/WRITE/DO

Keep a few things in mind as you begin the choice of losing your luggage. By keeping these things in mind, your life's journey will become much lighter and your path that much smoother.

1. **Judgment of Yourself**—Stop holding onto things from your past you've classified as mistakes. Lose the judgment of what you consider to be your past transgressions. You were never put here to get it exactly right one-hundred percent of the time. So, start by cutting yourself some slack.

2. **Judgment of Others**—While you're cutting yourself some slack, do the same for others. Lose the judgment of others. Don't judge one's past as being a determining factor for their future. After all, you have made mistakes; others have made mistakes as well. Learning to lose judgment and offering forgiveness instead is a way to clear the path for what your actually desire to be manifested.

3. **Express Your Desires**—Be clear with yourself and with God about what you truly desire. To be more specific, identify what you desire in the very moment you are in. When you are in the midst of a situation where you begin to feel the rising of angst, worry, doubt, anger, etc. immediately decide what you actually desire to feel and choose to begin to feel that way. By offering a more open and positive vibration, you create the reality you truly desire.

Chapter 9

Give Up the Struggle

"Once there was a man who hated his own shadow. When he walked, and found that his shadow was close behind him, he began to walk faster and faster. But the faster he moved, the closer his shadow came. So he ran like a madman. And in the end, he dropped dead. It is actually very easy to be rid of one's shadow—just rest under a tree. Just rest." — *Zhuang Zhou*

When considering 'giving up the struggle,' it may come across as completely contrary to the way we've been taught all our lives. It may seem almost blasphemous in its paradoxical connotation. Why would we ever give up the struggle? Isn't that what we're here for? Isn't this the way God ordained it to be? "Life is a struggle. No pain, no gain. Suffering is part of living. Never give up!" We've heard these clichés, internalized them, and made them truths in our lives. We've accepted struggle as simply part of the life cycle, and now we almost shun any life that is struggle-free. The thought of a no-struggle life seems contradictory to the way we've been conditioned. A no-struggle life is what fairytales are made of in our perceptions, therefore we don't trust the notion. So, what are we saying when we say 'give up the struggle?' What struggle are we suggesting to give up?

Giving up the struggle is giving up the struggle <u>against</u> life and going more with the <u>flow</u> of life and living. Give up the need to manipulate circumstances and events that are beyond our control (which is usually most of them). Give up the resistance associated with conditions surrounding life events. Stop fighting against a 'perceived' opposition. There is really only one opposition—you. You are often your greatest and only true opponent. And we tend to be very good at defeating ourselves.

By going with the flow of life and taking things as they come, addressing them from a place of inner peace, we discover that things only have the influence over us that we allow them to. Wayne Dyer said, "You are only one thought away from peace."

In Christian belief, I've heard a saying to "Let go and let God." Muslims may say, "Allah is the best knower." In Buddhism, there is a saying, "Letting go gives freedom, and freedom is the only condition for happiness."

Does any of this mean don't stand up for injustices or take action with regard to things we feel passionate and strongly about? No. Nor does it mean to passively put up with any negative or harmful situation you find yourself in and do nothing about it. By no means do these statements translate to roll over and just allow things to happen. This simply means to trust in a higher power that all things will work out as they are supposed to. Trust that things will happen in accordance to the infinite laws of the Universe that God has created and put in place. It means surrendering and yielding to, rather than opposing, the flow of life.

Certainly, this world has provided us all with many opportunities to fight and resist. We live in a world and a society where struggle, stress, strife, and suffering appear to surround us at every turn. There is possibly much we could and perhaps should be angry about and fight against. Whether it stems from our home lives with our families, our communities, our nation or the world as a whole, there appears to be ongoing conflict and adversity. There are apparent forces that seem to be in direct opposition to what's supposed to be good and right. There are many perceived social, political, and religious injustices taking place every day. There are many, many causes one could take up and be completely justified in fighting for. In 'giving up the struggle,' it is not meant to suggest that any action or stance you feel passionate about should not be addressed by whatever means you deem appropriate. But what we are suggesting is that you let any and all action start first with yourself and your mind.

Do you remember a game of Chinese finger cuffs many of us played as children? The object was to find an unsuspecting victim, have them slide their fingers through the woven bamboo contraption, and then figure out how to get free. The natural instinct was always to struggle your way out. Quickly you discovered the more you struggled the more you could not break free. The only way to free yourself was to relax and push your fingers with the tension as opposed to pulling against the tension which kept you stuck. Once you realized that, your fingers were soon free. The same holds true with quicksand or being in water. The more you fight against and struggle, the quicker you sink. The more you're able to relax and not panic, the greater your chances are for survival.

In this action-oriented world, we've been trained in the "more-effort, more-push to achievement" approach to life. We feel the need to "make" things happen. Hustle hard to achieve greatness, never realizing the greatest leverage is in alignment and being in oneness with God. **We forget that we are human BEINGS, not human doings.** We fill our days and lives with doing instead of being, which is where our greatest power lies.

So how do we give up the struggle, let go, and allow, while simultaneously inspiring change and standing up for what we believe in and are passionate about? For anything to ever change, no matter what it is, YOU must first be that change. You must see the change. Exemplify the change and project through your vibrational power the picture of your desire. **Envision and hold the thought in your mind's eye of the way you prefer the situation to be.** Let all inspired action come from a place of alignment BEFORE you take any physical action. Coming from any other place, the struggle will only continue. The "fighting against" approach usually only yields more of what you don't want. **What you resist usually persists.**

Example: There has been a war on terrorism and drugs forever. There has been a Palestinian and Israeli conflict forever. For every action, there is an equal and opposite reaction. It was Mother Theresa who, when asked why she never participated in anti-war demonstrations, stated, "I will never do that, but when you have a pro-peace rally, I'll be there."

When faced with a perceived struggle, ask yourself two questions:

1) How do I presently feel about this situation?
2) How does my inner being see this situation?

Then let your action be from a place of inspiration and alignment. Your aligned approach will feel good. It will feel right and non-emotional. Your action-oriented approach will feel anxious, angry, fearful, apprehensive, etc.

Remember: **Expectation + Belief = YOUR POINT OF ATTRACTION!** The Law of Attraction is absolute. What you emit will return. How you perceive things and what you expect will create your reality and, most importantly, has the power and potential to effectuate change in your world and the world abroad.

One person who is aligned is greater in power than thousands who are not. And one person can make a difference, start a movement, create a paradigm shift that causes the hearts of others to change by first exemplifying the change you want to see within yourself. Change your focus of struggle hard to spiritually focused energy for your desired outcomes.

THINK/WRITE/DO

Often, when we are faced with challenges, it is important to center ourselves first. Then act later. Centering ourselves is equivalent to planting your feet on solid ground, becoming stable, secure, and balanced before the next step is made. As we spoke about earlier in this chapter, there are two questions you want to ask yourself when faced with a struggle. These two questions are designed to help you become centered and grounded in your truth:

1. **How do I presently feel about this situation?**—Explore, acknowledge, and embrace what you currently feel about the situation. By exploring your feelings, without letting them take you over, you provide clarity of what is happening in the situation and this will help you identify which move you'd like to make next.

2. **How does my inner being see this situation?**—This question is designed to do the grounding. Keep in mind, our inner being is ethereal. Our inner being has authority over material things. Our inner being sees life authentically and is not moved by perception, ego, fear, worry, despair, or any other feeling of lack or inadequacy. Asking this question puts us in remembrance of that fact and provides for calm in the situation you are facing.

Chapter 10

The Paradigm Shift: Aligning Conscious Thought

Is it not wonderful to know that we create our own reality? We create our own fate, destiny, and livelihood. Learning to become unconditional lovers of life, not responding to every condition that pops up, but rather creating the life we desire for ourselves is the objective and purpose in life.

Thinking and moving about life with this thought process presents a shift in conscious thought—a paradigm shift. What is a paradigm and how can we use paradigm shifting to our greatest benefit, maximizing our greatest potential and experiencing the best version of ourselves possible?

Dictionary.com defines a paradigm as *"a framework containing the basic assumptions, ways of thinking, and methodology that are commonly accepted by members of a scientific community."*

A paradigm is simply how you view and think about things. It's your perception. It's the way you see the world. But it is a bit more objective than the subjectivity that personal perception provides. For example, someone stumbles into a store hazy eyed, with slurred speech, and acting belligerent, we could all objectively assume the person may be drunk, due to all outward appearances, when in actuality the person could have just taken some very strong pain meds that caused this behavior or could have some underlying physical condition we don't know about. It's our paradigms of how we have agreed a drunken person acts that gives us the deductive reasoning as to what's wrong with this person, not necessarily our personal perceptions.

Do you get angry or frustrated when someone zooms past you on the freeway at top speed possibly endangering your life and those around you? Do you have a zero tolerance of unruly children? How about you're at your favorite restaurant and right next to you are the most unruly children you've ever seen? They are running up and down the aisle, screaming, and, what's more, the parents seem indifferent to the situation? Or maybe you're at work and your co-worker just snapped at you in the most disrespectful way imaginable and you fire right back and give them a mouthful of thoughts and things you've been wanting to say for a long time?

What if you found out the person who zoomed past you had a dying child in the car; the family in the restaurant had just gotten news that their grandmother had just passed away; and the co-worker had just been fired by the boss?

Would your perception/assumption change regarding the behavior you observed initially? This is a paradigm shift. It causes you to look through a different lens. It's a change from one way of thinking to another. A paradigm shift in conscious thought can be a catalyst in facilitating authentic perception. It empowers us to move from where we presently stand in life to where we desire to be in our relationships, in our careers and businesses, and with our families.

Like most things, paradigms, in and of themselves, are neither good nor bad. They are neutral. If your paradigms are negative, they can keep you in a place of unfulfilled, going-through-the motion, passionless life experience. These types of paradigms create limiting beliefs and stifle conscious growth. Negative paradigms can keep you in perpetual bondage similar to being locked in a cell or held hostage by captives. Negative paradigms keep you held captive in your mind, which is where all true freedom resides.

Conversely, if your paradigms are positive, you experience happiness easily. Your outlook on life is one of optimism. You approach life's circumstances from a place of joy. Your expectations are aligned with your desired outcomes. Fulfillment is not a hope for you but a belief.

It stands to reason then that if you want different and better results in life, you should consider changing your paradigm, and that's the good news. YOU CAN CHANGE YOUR PARADIGM WHENEVER YOU CHOOSE! You have control over how you view this world and thus can restructure your destiny. How do you go about doing that?

THINK/WRITE/DO

Step one: Identify the negative paradigm. Ask yourself some tough questions about the most important things to you and where you are versus where you want to be. How do you feel about money, relationships, the economy, religion, politics, etc.? For example: "I have to work hard to be financially wealthy" or "It doesn't matter who's elected president, this economy won't get any better."

Step two: Tell a new and different story. You can use any tool at your disposal. Writing down positive affirmations, meditation, imagining, anything that you can use that shifts your mindset about a particular subject matter you wish to change. When the subject of money comes up whether from within or externally, let your responses be those that you desire your situation to be. The same with the subject of relationships, or any other subject matter. Speak ONLY of the desired outcome for which you want, e.g., "I have more than enough money to live comfortably" or "I am happily content with being by myself. However, when I do commit to a relationship, it will be all that I desire."

Step three: Allow room for the paradigm shift and be patient. As you take on these practices, create space for the subconscious mind to do its job and do what it does best, which is to help facilitate the desires, take orders, and assist you in achieving that which you want. Express your desires without time limits and ultimatums.

Just as it is now, where your conscious self may be moving negatively in some areas based off your sub/unconscious self, so it will be when the paradigm shift takes place. Your conscious self will move in the positive direction towards you desires whether you realize it or not. When your subconscious mind has been shifted to the bombardment of positive thought and expectation, you will begin to see that positivity manifested throughout your life in places you expect and in places you least expect.

Keep in mind we need to pay attention to our subconscious choices and common patterns of learned-thinking. Many of our choices are sub/unconscious. They can represent areas of learned behavior based on past experience. These areas should be investigated and evaluated. For example, if you've tried for success in certain areas but things did not work out the way you desired, you may harbor feelings of disenchantment, disappointment, emptiness, or frustration, or a feeling of being unfulfilled. Our scenario may look something like this:

Conscious thought—"I deserve the best."

Sub/unconscious thought—"Who am I to deserve nice things? I'm no different from other people."

Guess which paradigm is the more dominant? Yes, the unconscious paradigm/thought/belief. It could be called the sponsoring or parenting belief. It is the underlying *true* belief of what you *say* you believe. It is the belief that explains your current life status or present life experience.

Experiencing a conscious paradigm shift means that you know you see the authentic you. The authentic you is a co-creator with God. The authentic you operates from the core of your soul and not the surface of your circumstance. The authentic you is capable of manifesting all desires.

It is not necessary to get to the root of where the negative paradigm came from; why you think what you think, "Where did I get such an idea," etc. It doesn't matter where the negative paradigms came from… your environment, upbringing, socioeconomic status, etc. What is key to success in making a conscious paradigm shift is recognizing **where you are now, where you wish to be, and how to get there.**

Chapter 11
<hr>

Where the Unicorns Live

Since children, we have been conditioned to believe that happily ever after is somewhere in a far-off land. A wondrous place that is illusive and sometimes difficult for us to reach. We must set out on a quest in search of it. We must defeat all of the evil foes along the journey who stand in our way of finding this joy we seek. **The underlying message always seems to have us in search of**—in search of a higher, lighter, better state of mind. And we must fight and struggle to get there. Chasing rainbows to find the pot of gold. Finding four-leaf clovers for good luck. The world seems to be full of falsehoods with Prince Charmings, Snow Whites, Wicked Witches and Happily Ever Afters. Then at some point, after we've grown in age, we become disenchanted with the enchanted. We turn away from the world of possibilities and replace it with the world of improbabilities and label it as "reality."

Throughout *From Alignment to Enlightenment*, we will continue to discuss creating and holding the visions of your desires. We've spoken about the Law of Attraction and discussed vibrational markers and how we attract what we attract into our lives. We will share what CAN be and WILL be, depending on how you react, create and respond. For now, let's talk about where you currently stand. Your current state of mind. Your current "reality."

In my lifetime, I've been blessed. I have a tremendous drive for success and that has served me well in the corporate American environment where I earn money. (I am ONLY saying this to make a point. That is the only motivation here.) Anyone else looking at my life would agree that from what they can see, it looks like this man has made it to the top. His happiness, in the reality of his success, must be monumental. But what I have learned is, the best wealth for a person to have is living in his/her purpose in life. Therefore, happiness in life is determined not by quantity of material things but by quality of spiritual fulfillment. There is no happiness in material things. But there is true happiness in the sublime.

I had a conversation with my sister, who is another highly driven, career-oriented, successful person in corporate America. We talked about the epiphany of realizing we had been chasing the wrong things. We had both been chasing corporate success and promotion for years. Corporate success had been our motivating factors driving our perceived happiness in the workplace. The real epiphany is understanding that chasing corporate success in the name of finding ultimate happiness is the equivalent to chasing rainbows and looking for the pot of gold. It is equal to depending on four-leaf clovers and expecting good things to happen. It is comparable to searching for Prince Charming or Snow White with the expectation that once you find them, happily ever after is inevitable. It is the same as searching for unicorns.

In my personal experience, on every step up on the corporate ladder lies a fleeting hint of joy and happiness where I had anticipated sustained delight of my success. What actually comes next is the heavy burden of achievement, expectation, and output that may, **but most times does not**, align with who I truly am. Being in alignment with who I truly am also helps determine my true happiness. In other words, as the great poet Paul Laurence Dunbar said in one of his famous poems with a title so apropos, *"We Wear The Mask."* We wear the mask to assimilate with our environment having the false expectation of acceptance and happiness. However, we tend to become one with the mask, and, in turn, tend to hide who we truly are, which stifles our understanding of what we truly desire and what makes us truly happy.

So, how do we find our true happiness? First, we must stop depending on someone or some THING to measure our happiness. If you are depending on some person or something to measure your state of happiness, you will

ALWAYS come up short of the mark. The only thing we control in this world is how we feel and how we desire to feel.

Gratitude and happiness are forever linked. When determining your level of happiness on any given day at any given time in the midst of any given situation, acknowledge, speak and quantify your gratitude. In the midst of a tough situation, what are you grateful for? Your boss has you upset…. what good traits are there about him/her that you admire? Your significant other disappointed you…what are some of the things that person does that excites you in a positive way? You're angry about your lack of weight loss…. what positive things can you say about yourself that you are proud of?

Changing your focus will elevate your vibrational marker. As discussed previously, the Law of Attraction is absolute. Whatever you focus on is what you receive in return. We all emit vibrations as we are vibrational beings. Sound, light, electromagnetic waves, radio waves, microwaves, etc. all function in a vibrational way. As humans, our vibrational frequency is driven by thought, word, and emotion. Therefore, continuous focus on the negative begets more negativity. If your desire is to be happy, you have the ability to create that happiness instantaneously by adjusting your vibrational markers.

Identify one thing you are grateful for and focus on that thing. List all of the ways you are grateful for having that thing in your life. (HINT: It's even better when that "thing" is not manmade.) As you focus on what you are grateful for, you will feel a higher sense of happiness come over you. Being grateful and living grateful elevates your vibrational marker. Elevating your vibrational marker puts you more in line with who you truly are. Becoming more aligned with who you truly are allows for less resistance of your desires. Less resistance blocking your desires opens up the channels for you to receive your desires. Receiving desires that are aligned with who you truly are guarantees your TRUE happiness! This is not an exercise in suppression of emotion. Or a bombardment of positive thinking. This is the deliberate creation of happiness.

The reason material things don't bring happiness is because material things are fragile, shallow, and temporary. We thrive in the ethereal because we are ethereal beings. Why does walking along the beach, taking a jog outside or simply working in a garden make us feel a certain way? It is because we are closest with the one who created us when we do. We feel the comforts of our true home. When we continually pursue those things of material or things constructed of man or man's institutions in search of happiness, we will always fail our true selves. Our true selves delight in the non-material.

Find happiness in the crisp air of the winter winds. Become excited about the sun shining on your face. Be grateful for the unconditional love your pet brings to you. Discover joy in the simple fact that you woke up this morning and that you have a CHOICE of what type of day you decide to have. Choose to be happy and find something of joy in ALL things EVERY day. We cannot depend on things or others to determine our happily ever after. Happily ever after is happening constantly as long as you allow it. Say to yourself, "Today, I behold all of the abundance that surrounds me. The end of the rainbow is at my front door. My significant other and I ARE Prince Charming and Snow White. My front yard is FULL of four-leaf clovers. And the unicorns live in my back yard."

THINK/WRITE/DO

1. Find 15 minutes in your day, preferably in the morning, to sit quietly in your imagination. Imagine yourself living the best version of YOU. What are you doing? Who are you doing it with? Where are you while you're doing this activity?

2. Think of three things you are grateful for and write them down (preferably three things that don't cost money).

3. During your day, take time to allow your mind to drift and wander off to thoughts of the things you're grateful for and to the thoughts of the best version of you.

4. Do this several times, periodically throughout your day.

Chapter 12

Who Are You?

Have you asked lately who are you? Are you your name, your birthplace, your lineage, your personality, your demeanor? Who are you? Are you your status, your position, your aura, your disposition? Who? Are? You?

Fundamentally, you are your greatest desire. We oftentimes think of desires as carnal or materialistic wishes or aspirations. But your true desires come from within and generally have nothing to do with physical substance. Your true desires have everything to do with the alignment of you and your authentic purpose in being here. Finding out 'who you are' is finding out what your purpose is in this life at the same time.

> *"You are what your deepest desire is. As is your desire, so is your intention. As is your intention, so is your will. As is your will, so is your deed. As is your deed, so is your destiny."* — *Unknown.*

Understanding that we are the makeup of our greatest desires, and ultimately our greatest desires formulate our destiny, then it stands to reason that we should manage both our intention and our attention in life to align with our desire. By focusing our intention, we provide the fodder, the clay, the material that allows God, Allah, Jehovah, the Universe to co-create on behalf of our desires. Then it becomes necessary for us to focus our attention. God, Allah, Jehovah, the Universe finds ways to communicate with us on a daily basis. All we have to do is pay attention and follow the clues. Some people would call this communication, coincidence, happenstance, or good luck. I would call those terms nonsense. There is no such thing as coincidence. All things happen in order and for reasons.

> *"Coincidences are so much more than amusements. A coincidence is a clue to the intention of the universal spirit, and as such it is rich with significance."* — *Deepak Chopra*

I remember working for General Motors, September 2001. I was disenchanted with my career path. I didn't realize it at the time, but a series of events unfolded that I now understand as my intention and attention working in tandem with the Universe's need to fulfill my desires. My fundamental desire was to make an impact at the greatest level for my company. I didn't feel I was being allowed to do that to my potential. This was made clear to me during my annual review with my boss that September when he told me that my career goals were "too aggressive." My intention, at that point, was to seek out other opportunities at other automotive companies where my desire could be fulfilled.

Two weeks later, it "just so happened" I was having a conversation with a young dealer who had a dual store—Buick and Nissan. He asked me what my next move would be with GM. I shared with him that my boss had just told me that my career goals were "too aggressive." He laughed and said, "That's the GM way!" This dealer had a corporate contact at Nissan whom he called immediately as I sat in his office. The dealer told the Nissan exec about me and the things I had accomplished with General Motors. The next thing I knew, Nissan was flying me to their Regional Office for an interview. Even though my intentions were made known and the Universe was providing the "coincidence" to support it, my wife and I were still leery about Nissan because they had just come out of bankruptcy and they were a much smaller company than General Motors.

The interview went very well and I went back to Keene, New Hampshire, which is where we were living at the time. Keene, New Hampshire is one of the most remote places I've ever lived. The one-stop-light town is known for their annual Pumpkinfest during October. Every year, the town tries to break the Guinness World Record they have set every year for decades boasting the most pumpkins in a square block radius at one time. This particular October, the record was set at 22,633 pumpkins in the town square. The pumpkins were all carved with the most wicked faces and ghoulish expressions. It was amazing to see the incredible skill that artists put into carving the pumpkins. The town set up scaffolding four stories high to showcase all of the pumpkins, and Keene, New Hampshire once again broke the world-record for most pumpkins in a square block radius.

But my wife and I had a very real, jaw-dropping experience that day. We walked around the town square that October with the Nissan interview in the back of our minds along with the debate as to whether this was the right thing for us. In addition, things seemed more complicated because my wife also worked for GM at the time and we were concerned with how this would affect our income if I left—relocation, salary changes, her position with GM, the list goes on.

So, in the town square that had just broken a record of over 22,000 pumpkins in a square block, we walked right up on a pumpkin that sat on the 2nd level of the four-story scaffolding amongst 22,000 **that was carved out perfectly with the Nissan automobile logo!** In a sea of ghoulish faces and scary expressions for Halloween, here was a pumpkin simply carved with a Nissan automobile logo! My desire had been to be in an environment where my talents would be appreciated. My intention was to motivate to a company that would provide relief to my desire. My attention was in line when God, Allah, Jehovah, the Universe told me that this was the place for me to go! Via a pumpkin! I left General Motors the next week and went on to have an awesome experience working for Nissan for nine years.

Paying attention to the things we label as "coincidence" in our lives will help open the doors of your desires. This is one of the ways that God looks to communicate with us on a daily basis. We get lost in understanding WHO we truly are because "I've got bills to pay, a mortgage to meet and a job to do." But that's not WHO you are. Those are simply things you DO. Many of us have lost sight of who we truly are, thus losing sight of our true desires. So, by asking yourself, "Who am I?" and listening intently in the silence for the answer, the Universe will provide a better path to finding and living in your true purpose which will provide for authentic joy and happiness. Understand for yourself what your true desires are. Then set

every intention to live out your desires. Be limitless in your desire and in your intention. Lose all boundaries that hold you in place. From this point, PAY ATTENTION to circumstances as they unfold in your life. Take everything that you once labeled as "coincidence" and receive it as opportunity and confirmation.

Here's the real kicker. When you start to acknowledge those subtle things as not mere coincidences but more so opportunity and confirmation, THE MORE THEY WILL START TO UNFOLD FOR YOU! These opportunities come in small as well as large packages. The example I provided was a massive example. But sometimes they are more subtle. The important thing is to start recognizing them. Typically, we express desire, operate with intent and then ignore the synchronicity that supports the manifestation of those desires the Universe puts in our path. We don't recognize the gifts subtly being delivered because we're too busy "living life" and managing the rat race we've created. A more impactful way is to discover desire within yourself. Nurture and cultivate that desire. Then, watch it bloom in manifestation.

Operate in full intent while in alignment with your desire and expect it to manifest. Pay attention to the signals, the signs, the markers, the coincidences, the flukes, the chance encounters, the things that happen that support your desires and acknowledge them as they are happening. They all add up to your greater destiny.

Think about it like this…instead of seeing life as strictly linear cause and effect, understand your life as a symphony. A figurative symphony made up of countless instruments playing an infinite score that is the orchestration of your life where YOU are the conductor! God put the orchestra together but allows you to conduct the music. Write your music through your desires. Intend for your musical piece to be masterful. Listen attentively as it plays while you lead and direct the tempo to create the harmony that satisfies you. Rediscover who you are by discovering your authentic desires in this life, the things that make you happy yet have nothing to do with money or material things. Here, you will find yourself. From this place, develop your intent. Act on your intent. Then simply pay attention to the synchronistic symphony that plays the score of your life.

Chapter 13

The Package or The Product?

Have you ever noticed how companies use packaging to attract consumers? Ever noticed the designs of vodka bottles? The shapes of perfume bottles? Sometimes our final decisions are made based on what the package looks like. So what's more important? The package or the product? Do we fall in love with the package? Is the package the thing we covet? Does the package hold any **real** value?

I use this analogy to embark on a more somber subject...death. Or at least how we've come to understand the transition of life energy. When considering authentic purpose and perceptions, it is important to provide clarity regarding one of the most powerful events that happens during human life. But also understand that birth and death are opposite sides of the same coin. The power and meaning we give to them leads to the question...the package or the product?

I spoke with my mom some time ago and she told me that one of her co-workers "passed away" at the age of 51. My mom was very upset understanding that this young woman has left behind a husband and family. As I looked for words to help console her, I was drawn to help her understand our concept of death versus what is authentic reality.

"The absolute break between life and death is an illusion." — Deepak Chopra.

Our physical bodies have an expiration date. No question about that. But our souls are eternal. That is the beauty of life. Our bodies represent "the package" and our souls are "the product." What you value is not the package but should be the product. Is it not interesting to know that life is infinite? The soul is as boundless as the Universe and is one with the Universe and God the Creator at the same time. At a physiological level, hundreds of thousands of cells in our bodies perish daily only to be regenerated and given life again. This is how we continue to live. If our cells stopped dying and being regenerated, we would cease to exist. For example, dead skin cells are lost throughout the day and when we shower to allow new skin to live.

The body is recycled earth. Your thoughts are recycled information. Your soul is recycled energy. God, the Creator, Jehovah, Allah, the Universe is the founder and sustainer of life. So, in this context, death is a manmade concept as life is everlasting. Life perpetuates itself. And THAT is the miracle of all of God's creations.

Our thoughts, our emotions, our memories all operate at the ethereal level because they are a part of our soul. A doctor can't operate on your brain and find your thoughts, emotions, or memories. No scientist has ever dissected a human and found them. We mourn our loved ones and friends who transition because we do not "see" them in the same capacity as before, in an animated body, spending time in fellowship together on this physical plane. But the passing on of that person does not mitigate or stifle or negate the thoughts, emotions, or memories we have of that person. Therefore, we have not "lost" that person. We simply don't see them with our physical eyes. That person is not "dead" because we still commune with that person's soul with our thoughts, emotions, and memories. We still have the product.

Think about it like this…looking into the mirror provides us with a reflection. The definition of reflection is *"an image or representation of an object"*—Webster's Dictionary. An **image** or **representation.** So, in other words, what you see in the mirror is not your true, authentic self. It is a representation. Understanding that what we see is an image or representation suggests we are more than what we see. We are deeper than the reflection. The body is a representation of the authentic you that is your soul. The reflection is an image of the "package," but the "product" is what is of true value. The product should be our focus.

Are we spending enough time with our product? Or are we too concerned about our package? Granted, there is absolutely nothing wrong and it should be encouraged to take good care of our packages. Eating well, exercising, grooming, looking nice, etc., are all things that add value to our lives. No question. However, spending equal time with understanding the authentic you is just as if not more important—the you that you can't touch, see, or smell but you know is there. The you that resides within. Getting a better understanding of the you within will help you navigate through this life with incredible ease. It will also give you better perspective when another soul of like kind has moved on to a higher plane of life.

Understanding the true and authentic you as a powerful spiritual being, having co-creative power with God, which gives you power over material things, including your body, provides for a genuine understanding of the true you. So, you don't pass away. The package passes away. The product ascends to a higher plane of life because life is eternal. And death as we know it is an illusion.

Chapter 14

Us vs. Them

In the world today, and since the beginning of time for that matter, there has always existed some form of "us vs. them." Boundaries are clearly established, battle lines are drawn, exclusion is sought over inclusion, beliefs are passed down for generations, and the 'us vs. them' mentality is carried forward in perpetuity. But WHO are the "them" and WHO are the "us."

If you subscribe to this way of thinking, and we ALL do from time to time, whether subtle or overt, you must ask yourself, at which point do I become an "us" and at which point do I become a "them?" Either way, you will fall to one side or the other based on who is categorizing you at the time. Knowing that the "us" and the "them" is of subjective design, it cannot be deemed as fact, truth, or authentic. In other words, it is impossible to factually track an "us/them." We will prove this shortly. But for now, let's explore some of the more identifiable "us vs. them" scenarios.

African-Americans and Caucasians; men and women; Koreans and Japanese; police officers and black/brown people; Jews and Gentiles; homeless and wealthy; homosexuals and heterosexuals; citizens and illegal aliens; Crips and Bloods; Christians and Muslims; Israel and Palestine; Democrats and Republicans…the lists are endless of examples of the "us vs. them" mentality. But unlike a sporting event where there are teams who've established 'us vs. them' with a structured timeframe complete with rules, protocols, and processes, the "us vs. them" mentality of life is never-ending because it is perpetuated by belief. Belief is subjective to the

believer. Again…**belief is subjective to the believer** and we create our own reality from what we believe. Therefore, the simple notion of "us vs. them" in this context is moot and irrelevant to the definition of your life. Why? Because it is not fact. It is the perceptions we have adopted as fact. Us vs. them is an equation that nullifies itself on both sides.

$$x + y = z \text{ is the same as } z = x + y$$

On one side of the equation you will always be an "us." On the other side of the equation you will always be a "them." Even though the variables are switched around (us and them) they are still dependent on each other for the outcome. So if that is the case, the equation perpetually balances, meaning there is never a different factual outcome. I'm going to take a broad stroke. Let's say Palestinians hate Jews. To the Palestinian, the Jews are "them" and the Palestinians are "us." But if I was born in Israel, then the Palestinians are always going to be "them" and the Jews will always be "us." The beliefs that each of them hold are ironically dependent upon each other to perpetuity. Therefore, the equation will always balance with no different outcome although the parties involved (Jews and Palestinians) may believe a different outcome is possible if they continue their fight.

An enlightened understanding suggests not seeing the x or the y or the z as cause and effect but more so seeing the totality in the existence of the variables. The x, y, and z are **dependent** upon each other…**not independent** of each other. This is why "us vs. them" doesn't serve for any long-term meaning in our lives. Understanding the totality of the equation instead of determining a "right and wrong" side of it provides perspective and allows you to create a different outcome by introducing new variables.

Here's an example regarding race.

On November 8, 2014, *Newsweek Magazine* published an article entitled, "There Is No Such Thing As Race." They cited a 1950's scientific study. *"The United Nations Educational, Scientific and Cultural Organization (UNESCO) issued a statement asserting that all humans belong to the same species and that 'race' is not a biological reality but a myth. This was a summary of the findings of an international panel of geneticists, sociologists and anthropologists. There is no inherent relationship between intelligence, law-abidingness or economic-practices and race."* The article went on to say, *"However, over the past 500 years, we've been taught by an informal, mutually reinforcing consortium of intellectuals, politicians, statesmen, business and economic leaders and their books that human racial biology is real and that certain races are biologically better than others."*

Based on historical facts, we know that the early scholars, educators, and astronomers of the world believed that the earth was flat. They believed that if you set out on a ship, that eventually you would literally fall off the side of the earth and fall into oblivion. In fact, these people who believed so strongly in the flatness of the earth lobbied an "informal, mutually reinforcing consortium of intellectuals, politicians, statesmen, business and economic leaders" to support their positions for a very long period of time before groups of people began to gather to challenge what had been taught. Challenged what had been perceived as authentic truth. Challenged what was accepted as real knowledge. Challenged what the masses had been conditioned to believe.

The reasons why we perpetuate an "us vs. them" mental state is because we believe, have been taught to believe, and generally accept whatever those beliefs may be as truth. We decide that anyone coming against that belief invariably becomes a "them" to our "us." We lose sight of the authentic truth, which is the x, the y, and the z of our equations are not independent of each other but are dependent upon each other. The equation is inclusive. Not exclusive. We become closed to the fact that if we view the equation as equal parts, instead of parts separate from us, we can introduce new variables to the equation for overall desired outcomes instead of individual desired outcomes. We've lost sight of the fact that **whatever we believe and focus on expands**. Good or bad. When we collectively believe on something, the expansion is compounded. The Law of Attraction is absolute. What we focus on expands.

What would happen if masses of people began to believe that loving your 'perceived' enemy instead of hating your 'perceived' enemy would grant you immediate access to heaven? What if masses of people began to believe that showing compassion and understanding to "them" would help us all grow in enlightenment and peace? What if masses of people began to believe that the opinions, beliefs, and ideals of the "them" could actually help round out the vision and long-term expectations of the "us?" Again, whatever we believe and focus on expands. History supports this fact.

At some point in time, enough people in America believed that segregation and the mistreatment of people because of 'race' (which is a total fallacy) was wrong. Enough people generated a similar belief, which created a massive vibrational marker and thus attracted the desired outcomes of those who believed it! The Civil Rights Movement was born and aligned with the desires of all those who believed America could prosper in racial harmony.

Today, focus your beliefs on the fact that we are all part of the human race. Not the perceived 'race' divided by colors. Today, focus on the belief that showing and demonstrating love to EVERYONE will impart more love into the world. Like tossing a pebble into a lake and watching the ripples flow outward as far as they can. Today, focus your beliefs on the people we have deemed terrorists to find compassion, peace, and understanding from our demonstrated efforts of compassion, peace, and understanding. Believe it with everything you have and surround yourself with others who believe the same. Why? Because whatever you focus and believe on expands. And collectively, that expansion is compounded. Today, focus your beliefs on the fact that we are not independent variables designed to stand alone outside of other variables. But we are all dependent variables in an equation of life that is designed to balance itself in the whole. At the end of the day, there is no "them." There is **only** US.

Tend to and nurture your perceptions. Your true and authentic purpose is depending on you.

Energy and Emotions

Energy and Emotions...the Love Section

First and foremost, we are made up of energy. We are constantly vibrating. Same as music, light, radio waves, etc. We vibrate and energy is constantly in motion. Energy is produced, used, recycled, and used again... constantly. This is not metaphysical or theoretical. This is simply scientific fact. Often, we do not leverage the energy we possess. We tend to allow our circumstances or situations to determine our energy as well as our emotional state. Whether those are positive situations and circumstances or negative, we, often, "go with the flow" as opposed to directing the flow to where we would **desire** to go.

"Everything is energy and that's all there is to it. Match the frequency of the reality you want and you cannot help but get that reality. It can be no other way. This is not philosophy. This is physics." – Albert Einstein

Energy is created and used in restrictive circumstances as well as in circumstances that flow. For example, during a heated argument or debate, the energies that flow are of a restrictive nature, evidence being your capillaries restricting, which causes your blood pressure to rise. We become tense in our bodies, frowns may form on the face, and tension is present. Conversely, when we find something humorous and we laugh, energies flow without restriction. There is a sense of emotional freedom and openness. Sometimes it flows so much that you can't stop laughing, your belly hurts, and you cry because of the flow of energy being created and compounding upon itself. When allowed, energy compounds upon itself whether it is viewed as positive or negative. Energy doesn't care. The more attention you put on it, the more it grows. This is how debates turn to fights, how laughter turns to tears of comical joy.

One very important catalyst to how energy is restricted or how it flows is the emotion we carry. Our emotions are very powerful. Our emotions cause us to emit certain vibrational signals. Those signals are frequently contagious. As an example of how powerful emotions are, have you ever walked into a room where everyone is angry? Perhaps you were having a fantastic day and you walk into this space where every person you encounter is angry, frustrated, or irate? Or you come home to your spouse who's had a bad day and they are in a mood. How did you start to feel? At the very least, most would typically lose some of the happiness they were feeling. At most, you may begin to feel anger as your vibration looks to match the dominant vibrational frequency of the room. This does not happen at the conscious level of your brain necessarily. We sometimes lose our good moods and fall into melancholy, frustration, or anger while completely unaware as to why. The same holds true for when we interact with people who are in a joyous mood. If we walk into a space where we've been having a very bad day, yet everyone else in the room is happy, smiling, laughing, and conversing with upbeat and up tempo emotion, we tend to begin to resonate with that vibrational frequency.

The beauty of understanding how energy and emotions work in harmony is understanding that we have the innate ability to direct this energy and manage our emotion. This is important when understanding HOW to manifest our desires in this life. Energy and emotion play a key role in alignment, which we will discuss in the next section. The most powerful emotion and the foundation of all emotions is love.

When operating from a foundation of unadulterated love, we offer no resistance, no restriction, but instead openness that allows energy to flow. Better yet, it creates an open space for our desires to flow freely without restriction. Directing and managing the intention of our emotions creates a powerful energetic vibration specific to you and your desired outcomes in this life.

Chapter 15

The Eternal Guidance System (EGS)

Most of us have some form of Global Positioning System (GPS) on our cell phones and/or in our vehicles. Some of them are highly sophisticated and able to perform very intelligent functions. But the point is simple: Calculate the route to get from where I am to where I want to be. If you notice, the system doesn't ask or even care where you've been, what the weather is today, where you were yesterday, or what mood you're in. The GPS is only concerned with where you are now and where you want to go, with greater emphasis on the latter.

So it is with our Inner Being. One of its main benefits is providing us with clear direction, particularly when we've lost our way. It is our own personal internal or should we say eternal guidance system (EGS). Similarly, it knows the clear path from here to there; however it depends highly on us knowing where we want to go. Our eternal guidance system knows the best route to move from confusion and struggle to clarity and ease; to shift out of worry and frustration and into confidence and peace. But we must have clear vision. Or at least clarity and understanding of what we want and deserve to feel good and be happy.

As babies, we use this system so well. We cry when we are hungry, sleepy, thirsty, or uncomfortable and, for the most part, our needs are met rather quickly. We laugh, coo, and show our pleasure readily. We know exactly what we want in any given moment and how to get it. It is only as we grow and learn the so-called ways of the world from those around us (parents, teachers and society) that our innate guidance system usually falls to the wayside, buried deep within us and rarely called upon. However, it is still there, much like a dormant GPS system, ready to be plugged in to the energy source to accurately direct us on our impending journey. If only we would recognize it, call upon it, and trust it! Many of us learn later in life (or should I say "re-learn") how to access this power. Once we begin trusting on our "EGS," it gets easier and easier and the guidance gets clearer and clearer.

So what happens when we lose the path or can't find the highlighted route? And how do we utilize our God-given gift of internal guidance? How many times do we have a feeling of dread or discord within us, warning us not to do something, and yet we do it anyway and discover it was not really a good course of action, and we should have trusted our intuition? It's easy to use the electronic GPS and have faith in the system because you can physically SEE your progress. You're moving, so you know for certain you're getting there. When we use our EGS, however, we may not be able to 'see' our progress right away because it is vibrational progress. Things in our lives manifest almost entirely on a vibrational level before we see any physical manifestations. We know we are on the right path by the way we FEEL. Our emotions are our best indicator as to whether we are in alignment with our Inner Being and therefore on the right path.

It's time we began to trust our own feelings again, and listen to our own personal guidance systems. Every one of us was born a complete master of our Eternal Guidance System. We all have access to it, if we only take heed.

THINK/WRITE/DO

Here are three ways to get started.

1. **Trust**—Have faith that you have an *eternal guidance system* inside you.

2. **Exercise**—Build your guidance system muscle by talking to it, testing it, and tuning into its answers.

3. **Love**—Trust that your guidance system is love-based. It speaks the language of your soul.

Try following these three techniques to help learn how to trust and follow your own inner voice. The more you do it the more natural it will become.

Chapter 16
=============

Lose Control

Often, I find myself looking to control a situation. To affect a different outcome. To steer the situation to my direction or favor. To influence another to do what I want them to do. To control the reality I see. My "perceived" control tends to drive me. But recently, I heard Esther Hicks say, "The speed of accuracy is the absence of resistance." THE SPEED OF ACCURACY IS THE ABSENCE OF RESISTANCE. When you consider control, it implies a regulation to manage resistance. But in the absence of resistance is accuracy. So is it better to release our perceived control and be open for allowance to flow? Yes. And that doesn't mean we readily accept an unwanted situation, circumstance or behavior. As we will discuss, creating a space for allowance clears a path for what we truly desire to be manifested. Therefore, the more we look to control a situation, the less control we truly have because of the presence of resistance.

In a simple way, we all look to have control to achieve our desired result. But the bottom line is, all we need to do is desire and allow. Allowance offers no resistance. Allowance offers no restriction. Therefore, energy and emotion are 'allowed' to flow freely. ALLOW things to happen freely and naturally. I know that is very counterintuitive. We have been conditioned to stand up for what we feel is right; fight, if we must, for what we believe in; and dominate the space we're in. But perhaps we should stop looking to control the outcome. Because the more we do, the further our desired outcome runs away from us. For example, if you're chasing money it runs really fast. If you express your desire to have it, and hold your vision in alignment with your desire, it will come to you. You will not need to chase it. That doesn't mean you don't act on your desires. It means instead of putting your desired outcomes on a deadline full of ultimatums the way we do, simply desire and allow. When we desire and allow, we must KNOW it will be given. The Law of Attraction is hindered and sometimes halted by resistance. Control and resistance are two sides of the same coin.

I am a firm believer that everything happens for a reason. There are no coincidences. Life is one gigantic orchestra. And God has put the Universe in place to orchestrate it all. That's why we are in the right place at the right time, ALL the time. But what we have sometimes forgotten is that we are spiritually empowered by God in this world to manifest our physical desires—the desire to be a successful mother or father, or successful in sports, or your career, or as an office manager, a painter, or whatever pleases you. So instead of focusing on and looking to control a problem, we should simply start manifesting solutions. Manifest your desired outcome by expressing your desire and watching the Universe put people and things in your path that align with that desire. Everything that is physical is a manifestation of consciousness. The beauty of this world is that we are all designed and created to be **deliberate creators**. Lose the perceived control. Desire. Allow. Know. Receive.

THINK/WRITE/DO

Do you tend to want to exercise some type of control over most things in your life? (No judgment here as many of us fall into this category.) Here's a way to begin to forego the need to be in control.

1. Grab a sheet of paper and draw three columns. In the first column, write **Complete Control**. In the second column, write **Moderate Control**. In the third column, write **Some Control**.

2. Pick one situation, circumstance, or person you feel the need to control and write that under the appropriate heading depending on your degree of control, e.g. your children may go under Complete Control while your marriage may go under Moderate Control and your business may go under Some Control. Remember, just pick one thing for each column. These are the things that give you the most angst when you are not exercising some type of control over them.

3. At the bottom of the page under each column, write down your desired outcome of that thing you feel the need to control. What is your single most focused desired outcome for the situation you look to control? e.g. If you are having financial troubles, your authentic desire is not to win $1 million dollars in the lottery. Your authentic desire is to be financially abundant. If your business is struggling, you're looking for your business to become self-sustaining and successful.

4. After you've written down the three things you look to control most at the top and your authentic desired outcome of those things at the bottom, write down what you think will happen if you release your control under each column head. What is it that you anticipate will happen if you shift your focus from your perceived control? Exhaust the list of what you believe will happen. Will your kids turn on you? Will things fall completely apart at work? Write it down.

5. Now you should have your three columns—Complete, Moderate and Some Control—the list of things you think will happen if your release control, and at the bottom of each column should be your desired outcome.

6. Now that you've completed this, the real work begins. Every day, read what you have written in the Complete Control column. Then read the first thing you think will happen if you release control. Then read the desired outcome. Focus your energy on the desired outcome. Read the first thing you think will happen again. Then the desired outcome. Do this again and again. Allow yourself to focus less on the anticipated outcome and more on the desired outcome. Do the same with the other two columns as well.

Do this every day. You will begin to change your focus and expectations. You will begin to lose control. Losing control in the best possible way will, in turn, deliver your most desired outcomes. Take your time and be easy on yourself. It may be easier by starting with the Some Control column as the anticipated outcomes in this column may be easier for you to release.

		Complete Control	Moderate Control	Some Control
Step 1	**Level of Control**	**Children**	**Marriage**	**Business**
Step 3	**What I think will happen if I relinquish my perceived control**	My children won't behave properly	He will stop paying attention to me	My business will fail
		They will be unruly	She won't love me the way she should	No one will buy my products
		They won't have discipline	He will think I don't care	The competition will beat us
		They will grow up to be criminals	She will always get her way	We will be unsuccessful
		They won't be responsible	He will think he won	We will go bankrupt
		They won't be successful in life	She will find someone else	We will be on welfare
		They will go to prison	He will cheat on me	Life will be horrible
Step 2	**Desired Outcome**	My ultimate desire is for my children to grow up to be productive, responsible adults.	My ultimate desire is for my spouse and I to have the best marriage possible.	My ultimate desire is for my business to be self-sustaining and successful.

Chapter 17

Vibration Basics

"Everything in life is vibration." — *Albert Einstein*

What is vibration? How does it work? And why is understanding it so critical?

When we think of vibration in its basic form, we think of something shaking or oscillating. Simply put, vibration is energy in motion. If you've taken a chemistry class, you probably remember learning about atoms, and that everything is made up of atoms. These atoms are in a constant state of motion, and depending on the speed of these atoms, things appear as solid, liquid, or gas. Sound is also a vibration and so are thoughts. In a vibrational Universe, one vibration often influences another. For example, when struck, one bell in a room full of bells will generate a sympathetic response from all of the bells attuned to that note. Another example is a dog howling when it hears a sound or tune; it is trying to match the frequency it is hearing. It has been proven that a more powerful vibration influences a weaker one.

Our emotions create positive and negative vibrational markers for us in communicating within the Universe. We can see evidence of the power of positive emotion in our history as one person in alignment (positive vibration) can have greater power over many who are not in alignment (negative vibration), e.g., Martin Luther King Jr., Mahatma Gandhi, and Mother Teresa. Therefore, the adoption of a positive vibration must inevitably sublimate or redirect a lower one with sustained focus.

We live in a vibrational Universe. Matter, energy, and thought are fundamentally vibrational in nature, so that each interfaces with the other in a subtle, but powerful way. Given this understanding, we may then apply the physics of vibrational interaction to the relationship between the nonphysical and the physical world in everyday life.

There has been interesting research conducted that proves every single beat of your heart sends out an electromagnetic, 360-degree spherical bubble at the speed of 186,300 miles per second, roughly about the same speed of light. Think about that. We are all magnetic fields constantly sending out a frequency. Why is this important to note? Couple our physical vibrational frequency with our mental vibrational frequency and the Universe is responding always to those frequencies, which are powered by our emotions. So we emit the frequency through our physical heartbeat, thoughts, and emotions. The Universe then tries to match or respond to that frequency, thus giving back to us, in direct proportion, that which we are vibrating. Our vibration is a means of communication with the Higher Power, and the Law of Attraction is responding to our vibration. Therefore, it becomes critical to pay attention to how we feel, the mood that we choose to sustain, and the thoughts we allow to dominate our minds, because there is always a corresponding/reciprocating response from the Universe.

Be careful, therefore, with thoughts, as it is our thought and emotion (vibration) that create the reality we experience. We do not *attract* what we want, we *attract* what we are.

Chapter 18

Loving Unconditionally

What does loving unconditionally mean to you? For most I've talked to and come in contact with, it means you love me regardless—regardless of my flaws, regardless of how I treat you or how I behave. We're taught early on about agape love and the love of God being unconditional. We've been taught to trust in agape love as being the ultimate, the epitome of happiness, nirvana, the 'happily ever after.'

I used to be a stark skeptic on the subject, having been through many failed relationships. I was even cynical towards the idea. I now better understand what unconditional love is about. Unconditional love does not mean you look at some despicable behavior and love it anyway. And it's not so much about loving the other regardless of their treatment of you. Unconditional love is more about loving YOURSELF. Loving yourself enough to stay in alignment with your inner being and connection to your Source (God) despite the condition. It's more about your commitment to holding yourself in vibrational alignment, your unyielding relationship between you, the REAL you, and God.

Your Creator loves—PERIOD! Not because of anything that we do or *don't* do. There's nothing particularly special about us in that sense that God would love us, as God loves ALL creation. But choosing to demonstrate that level of love to each other the way God does…seeing each other through the eyes of God, noncritical, nonjudgmental, not depending on a person's behavior nor condition of a thing to change…THAT is what unconditional love represents.

Unconditional love is saying that I want so much to be connected to God energy that I will allow the fullness of who I really am to flow through me no matter what you do or say, no matter what thing happens. Of course it does not mean tolerate abuse or behavior that is demeaning or degrading. But how easy is it to love the lovable? And how much more difficult is it to love those people and situations that are not so easy to love? This is the point of loving your enemies and turning the other cheek. You can't just look at someone with absolute love in your being without them coming into alignment with the absolute love in your being. This is the way we uplift the world. To love unconditionally, not because the thing or person is **lovable**, but because lovable is in **you** now and is your eternal way.

Love is our fundamental function. That's why it feels so good to love and to be loved. If you don't believe that, ask yourself what tops that feeling from an emotional standpoint? Nothing. It is our most fundamental emotion and is needed for survival. However, we tend to put parameters on love, which means we put parameters on ourselves. Release your love. Release it to be free to roam and explore new heights. Imagine yourself walking through life with love as your primary emotion. It is primary when you grocery shop, walk the dog, go to work, pay your mortgage…infuse LOVE in ALL things you do to unleash the ultimate joy, happiness, peace, and of course…love. After all, it is your eternal way.

THINK/WRITE/DO

Make four conscious decisions to love unconditionally.

1. Decide to love yourself enough to not sacrifice your alignment for anyone or anything.

2. Decide to love without any expectation of love's return.

3. Decide to see the beauty and value in all things.

4. Decide to **love more by "caring" less.** This sounds contradictory. Yes, you want to "care" for a person in the sense that you strive for their well-being and happiness. However, you don't want to "care" in the sense that your love is predicated and governed by specific outcomes, which, by definition, would be conditional.

So, not: "I don't care what you decide [because your well-being is irrelevant to me]."
but instead: "I don't care what you decide [because I just love you regardless of your choices and actions]."

Don't love in return for actions that make you happy. Derive happiness from the act of loving unconditionally.

Chapter 19

Is That Your Primary Desire?

In this fast-paced world of acquiring things, making an income, and staying "ahead," we have to remind ourselves constantly of aim and purpose. It's really about fulfilling our purposes and giving meaning to our lives. All of us have similar aspirations generally speaking—to live better and healthier lives, to prosper and thrive, to achieve, etc. And we all have given our own subjective definitions to what this means and how we should go about attainment.

In a conversation I once had, I shared some goals I have and things that I had been working on that are now coming into fruition. I was asked the question. "Is that your primary desire?" Meaning, was it the thing I desired most or could I be settling for a secondary desire. I felt this to be a good moment for introspection and it offered questions I had to find answers to.

Am I living and fulfilling my primary desire—what I want most in life? Not to say that a secondary or less desirable thing is not worthy of our attention or does not have noble outcomes that warrant our involvement. But is the secondary desire really and truly getting you closer to that thing you desire **most?** And if not, what call to action are you inspired to do?

Many times, we think that "purpose" or "desire" is definitive, meaning it has to be a concrete approach with no ambiguity, and with clear, concise objectives for attainment. This often causes anxiety and frustration because you may not have all the answers to exactly what your purpose is in this life, or even what you truly desire. I've asked many people, "What is it that you desire for your life? What is it that you really want to do? What makes you happy in doing it?" Often the answer is a resounding, "I don't know." And that's okay!

We take in all this information and read books written by highly regarded writers that suggest we must absolutely and unequivocally know what our purpose and/or desires are; that we must have a clear vision. And on the surface this makes sense, right? Because "if you don't know where you're going how can you get there?" It seems we would be as Earl Nightingale put it, "ships on an ocean without a rudder, just moving about aimlessly, whichever way the wind blew." So we scramble around from one thing to the next looking for and trying to discover our purpose and trying to figure what we truly desire. Sometimes, we also get lost in whether this is our own desire or someone else's. These patterns lead us to become discontent with where we are in life.

This is where we propose paying more attention to being in **alignment** and focusing more attention on your **vibration** than anything else. Why? Because in your alignment, your purpose becomes clear. Your desires become clear. What you were put on this earth to do becomes clear. CLARITY becomes one with you and your way of being, which is one of God's gifts to us all.

In the book *The Alchemist* by Paulo Coelho, the main character Santiago strikes out on what he thinks his mission and purpose is in life; "his personal legend," as referred to in the book. But on his quest, he discovers that what he thought to be his main desire has changed through the course of his journey. His ultimate purpose was only revealed to him later after he'd been on the journey for some time. By simply following his bliss and acting on the things that made him happy, his purpose was revealed. He initially just made the **decision to act**. You don't have to have an identified purpose at this very moment for your purpose to be working towards manifestation. What is important is following your bliss, your happiness, and what feels right and in alignment with your soul. The main thing is making a choice and getting in alignment with that choice. The Universe will handle the rest.

I've spent time in the healthcare industry as an Occupational Therapist. People asked me all the time, "What is that? What exactly do you do?" My answer: I make people feel better. Is my purpose in life to be an OT? No, this was a method to assist me in fulfilling my purpose, which may change overnight or I may even have several methods for attainment of the ultimate desire.

Often my answer is, "My purpose is to serve my community and to leave people I encounter better off than they were when I met them." Taking a more general approach will open up various avenues of fulfillment for you. Spend time thinking about things important to you. What are some of your values? What things really get you going? If you draw a blank, fine. Get in alignment. Be present in your now moment, meaning wherever you are at this point in life is all right. Be alright with it, while at the same time desiring more. Not necessarily desiring more things, but more clarity. Dissatisfaction brings about change. Spend time appreciating the job or current business that you don't like. Demonstrate gratitude now, even in the midst of discontent.

How can you be sure you are fulfilling your desire and purpose? How does it feel to you? Remember your Eternal Guidance System (EGS). It will let you know right away where you are. Are you stressed? Does your work bring you angst or anxiety, frustration, agitation, or feelings of unworthiness? Then you know you're out of alignment and that you are probably not fulfilling your true mission in life. When you are doing what you were meant to do, IT FEELS GOOD! It feels like ease and comfort. It's energizing!

So take an account of where you are right now in life. If you're happy and feeling good, keep doing what you're doing. If not, take a deep breath, get still, and ask, "What is it that I should be doing?" and then start moving, keeping your eyes and ears open as your answers are revealed.

Chapter 20

What Is Learned From a Mother's Love?

We've touched on a couple of different aspects of love. As presented, love operates as a fundamental emotion to all other emotions. It is our primary desire as a newborn child. We can expect more love to come our way as we freely offer love to others. But what can we learn from the love of a mother? And what does a mother's love teach us as children that we should never forget as adults?

Thank God, Allah, Jehovah, the Creator, Yahweh, the Universe, the Almighty for the miracle of motherhood. The Almighty has given women the miracle of carrying life along with the innate ability to love and nurture unconditionally. Mothers love in spite of. Mothers provide leadership, guidance, and protection. Mothers are sounding boards to the rationale of life. Mothers provide direction and sustenance, nourishment for the body, as well as for the soul. Mothers provide support. Mothers are consistent and unwavering. Mothers are in perfect tune with nature. Mothers ARE nature incarnate—birthing life through their love, creativity, and long-suffering. Mothers help complete the cycle of life.

While not all women are mothers, this does not exclude those who do not have children from possessing and displaying the same innate qualities of motherhood. The loving, nurturing, compassionate, guiding, directing, teaching, patient characteristics of motherhood are often shown in women who have never had children. How is this possible? How can this be? Is it simply the way God created women in the first place? Or is it learned behavior that women are socialized to act and react in certain ways? Maybe it's both. Nevertheless, there are lessons for all of us to learn from this.

When we speak of ALIGNMENT, we speak of those actions taken that put us at the greatest point of happiness and love, the place where you experience perpetual joy. The ENLIGHTENMENT we speak of has everything to do with the acute awareness of all things. Enlightenment equates to an authentic understanding of all things. It is your true reality, the place where you truly understand yourself. It is understanding your co-creative power within this material world. One does not come without the other. Therefore, align to enlighten. We will discuss this in depth later. When considering "the road to enlightenment" (we put this in quotes because there is no road, it simply is), one of the main beginning points is surrender. It is the surrender of many things that we feel have made us who we are. The reason for this surrender is to release the inauthenticity that has created the **ego** we consider to be our being or who we consider ourselves to be. This is not the easiest of tasks. But it is necessary if true alignment and enlightenment are expected.

According to Deepak Chopra, surrendering for enlightenment includes, "full attention, appreciation of life's richness, opening yourself to what is in front of you, non-judgment, absence of ego, humility, being receptive to all possibilities and allowing love." When I consider my mother and how she treats me, I see clearly how she demonstrates the same attributes regarding enlightenment. My mother provides me her full attention when I ask. She considers the richness of life as any time we are able to spend time together, and especially with her grandchildren. She takes things as they come and remains open without judgment but rather meets me with encouragement. My mother, while knowing her self-worth, does not display or get caught up in ego and would never let ego determine her direction. She walks with confidence yet remains humble and displays humility. She has always been open to the possibilities of life even when being faced with life's adversities. And she has accomplished all of these things by giving and allowing love to flow at all times.

Granted, all mothers are not created the same. But understanding the sacrifice and the true selfless acts of mothers in general is enough to know that a mother's love comes from an enlightened place. These innate attributes God has given to women in general provide a view of enlightenment for not only the children they bear but also for all people of the world.

Imagine a world where every human offers full attention to the moment in which we are experiencing whatever life has to give. We would live in that moment, experiencing all it has to offer and then create the next moment and do it all over again. Instead of being caught up in planning out the far future, spend time in the right now with your full attention the same way a mother provides that full attention to that child in need.

Imagine a world where you cherish and appreciate life's richness. Wealth is found in the small fleeting moments that we tend to take for granted. Find appreciation and gratitude in the things money is not designed to pay for.

Open yourself to what is in front of you. Don't resist it, but allow it to flow, finding whatever is happy within the situation, even if it is a tough state of affairs. Challenge yourself by focusing on whatever is positive in the midst of the challenging situation. Continue to leverage what you are grateful for in that moment.

Release judgment. Nobody on Earth lays ownership to a heaven or a hell. Release the judgment you levee against yourself and against others. At any given moment, we have a choice to create another moment. Don't dwell on your past or another's past. Those experiences are a culmination of moments. Create new moments and simply live and let live. These are the ways we operate in alignment while creating and manifesting our heartfelt desires.

While you're at it, release your ego. Self-worth and self-confidence are valued. Ego is worthless in regards to enlightenment. Ego lives for itself and only for itself. Ego lives for the betterment of ego and will direct your true self down a road of self-gratification and self-praise. Let your ego go free and keep your self-worth.

Remain humble. One of the ironies of aligning to enlightenment is you will achieve greatness beyond your imagination. But you will not relish the greatness you've achieved and have also desired. In other words, in order to achieve the greatness you desire, you must remain humble. And even after you've achieved the greatness you desired, you will keep your humility.

As stated, truly live in the moment. Because at any given moment, you have the ability to create another moment. Therefore, being receptive to all possibilities provides a blank canvas for you to create whatever that next moment will be. Realize you have been created without bounds and the Universe is abundant.

The gas to make it all go is allowing this with love. Love is where we come from. Love is who we are. Love satisfies all things. Love provides the vehicle that propels our desires and our happiness, and provides fullness for our souls. It only happens with love.

These things are the attributes of motherhood, understanding that motherhood is a state of mind and not only a definition of women with children. But in this world, we have an opportunity to nurture, provide leadership, exercise patience, offer moral sustenance, be consistent and unwavering, and endow guidance, direction, and support, all wrapped in unconditional love. This is the same love a mother has for a child. THIS is the same love that fuels and propels alignment with oneself for gratified enlightenment and authentic understanding for and of the world.

So, as we look out on the world today, let us examine and understand what we may learn and what can be applied to everyday life from a mother's love.

THINK/WRITE/DO

What is learned from a mother's love? Perhaps authenticity? Enlightenment? Love? All of those things apply. To keep it in perspective and applicable to your daily walk, we encourage you to think about and consider the following:

- **Be in the Moment**—Offer your full attention to the person in front of you, mentally and physically.
- **Find The Greatest Appreciation in the Smallest Things**—Look to be appreciative in those small things that money can't buy.
- **Be in a Constant State of Allowance**—Whatever tough situation you are faced with, do not resist what is happening. This does not mean you like it or are physically harmed by something. But opening yourself up in the midst of tough or hard situations and circumstances means seeking out what is positive in the situation and focusing your energies on that while leveraging positive expectations.
- **Release Judgment**—By releasing judgment of both yourself and of others, you create an open space for your authentic desires to be realized. Holding judgment implies resistance. Wherever there is resistance, there is restriction of movement. Release judgment and find freedom.
- **Mitigate Ego**—We will go in depth regarding ego a little later in this book but for now, just know that our egos tell us stories of embellished half-truths as opposed to authentic facts. Be aware of this and just be sure to manage the ego. Not too much and not too little.
- **Remain Humble**—If the ego is in check, it makes remaining humble much more easy. What's ironic is, the humbler we remain the more our desires are realized because we have taken our energies and focus off of the "thing" that puffed up our egos and placed those energies and focus on being in a state of appreciation, gratefulness, and humility...the greatest cocktail for success in this life.

Chapter 21

What's Love Got To Do With It?

No one can deny the power of Tina Turner's song "What's Love Got To Do With It" from the 1980's. Tina goes on to say, "what's love but a sweet old-fashioned notion?" But the reality is, love has **everything** to do with it. Love has everything to do with all things. And it's not just about romantic love. It's about agape love. Loving unconditionally. Loving without judgment or prejudice. It's about loving in spite of the circumstance. Love is where we come from. But oftentimes, we measure our love to give us direction on whether or not we **should** love or if someone **deserves** the love we have to share. Sometimes, these are the "scales" we tend to "weigh" our significant others on as well. "Oh, I will love you if you do 'this' but if you do 'that' I won't love you" is how we tend to behave.

In 1971, an R&B group called The Persuaders had a hit song entitled "Thin Line Between Love and Hate." I'm sure many of us can relate to the emotion and perceived reality of the song. But how is it that the line can be so thin? How is it that people spend thousands of dollars for elaborate ceremonies in the name of love and shortly thereafter fight to the death in a court of law admonishing hatred for the one they vowed to love forever? What happened to the butterflies in the stomach, the fireworks in the sky, and the long late night talks? How is it that all of those feelings are traded for disdain, hatred, and indifference? And who is in 'control' of all of this emotion? It was scary, yet exhilarating, to be out of control when the feelings of passion, adoration, and love flowed so rich and intensely. But people become so matter-of-fact and assured when those feelings turn sour, as if the feelings of love never existed in the first place. How is it that we can be so entirely juxtaposed in our emotion? Perhaps we're all a little schizophrenic. Maybe. But we believe there's a much better understanding that should be realized.

Do you remember your first time falling in love? Can you recall all of the openness and freedom you felt? All of the passion and feelings of, 'everything is perfect with the world?' You knew that as long as that person was around you felt safe and confident. As long as you and that person were together, you could conquer the world. There was nothing that the two of you could not handle or do, as long as you were together. Feelings of happiness and joy were a part of your everyday outlook. But later things changed. "He doesn't look at me the same anymore." Or "she gets so upset about the smallest things." Or "Yeah, I love him. I'm just not IN love with him." Or "I hate it when she does xyz!" The person you are with has not changed fundamentally. Yet, how is it that we didn't see these things before that we are so critical of now? Where were these traits and characteristics when we were planning our wedding? How did we not see this person for who they really are? Where did the love stop and the hatred start?

The issues, the problems, the anger you feel, and the frustrations ALL reside within **yourself**, not the other person. The fact is, true fulfillment comes from within, NOT from without. So in other words, happiness flows from the inside out and not from the outside in. Oftentimes, we look to the other person to provide our happiness, but we are often disappointed in what they deliver. We are unhappy because the other person failed to make us happy. We are looking for solutions to our problems in another person whereas all the solutions we seek are within ourselves. The absolute beauty of this is the fact that at any given time, we have the ability to align our desires from within and expect the result we create. The **only** thing we control in this world is how we **feel**. At any given time, we have the ability to feel whatever we choose to feel, absent anyone else.

The Love/Hate scenario plays out for specific reasons. It comes down to something simple—allowance and resistance. When we express our desires and allow them to flow, **things come naturally and in the created time that will best fit your life**. When we resist, or attempt to control our outcomes or control other people, our experiences go against our desires. Resistance, judgment, and ego all facilitate inner turmoil that is manifested in argument, disappointment, and debate. Think about being head over heels in love with your significant other. Usually there is an emotional sincerity that exhibits very little judgment. You are wide open to any and all possibilities with this other person. The heightened state of allowance provides a vehicle for your emotional bliss. You experience love in its purest form.

As we continue in our relationships, we all come to expect certain things. We weigh the other person on our emotional scale and when they don't line up with our expectation of keeping us happy in a particular area, we hand down the verdict. "You are WRONG! YOU are not making ME happy!" All the while, the ego you seemingly let go back when you were 'in love' has come back with a vengeance and will not be denied a seat at the table. Your ego is what tells you that you have to prove your point. You have to 'win' the argument. You MUST come out on top in the situation. We hold onto these egotistic feelings of judgment against the other for not helping us be satisfied with ourselves.

The authentic reality will tell us that it doesn't matter who is "right or wrong" in the situation. The authentic feeling we desire is love. Period. However, during a heated debate, we sometimes lose sight of the foundation of our relationship: love. We sometimes lose sight of love because the behavior our significant other is demonstrating does not suggest love. Their behavior may suggest disdain, selfishness, hatred, inconsideration, etc. But does that negate what is foundational in your relationship? Was your relationship based on disdain, selfishness, hatred, and inconsideration? Did they set out to not care about you? Or did they choose to care about themselves more, at that time, than they chose to care about you? This is not to say relationships don't have trials, challenges, and tribulations. But when you are in the midst of your relationship challenges, take the complete onus off the other person and decide what you want to feel. Then choose to assess, allow, and love. In other words, when you're doubting if the love you know is alive in your relationship or if the other person is not responding or acting the way you've deemed as plausible, simply ask yourself, "Does he/she love me based on the overall history of things and actions they have demonstrated?" If yes, then what are you really upset about? If the answer is no, then make another decision that will bring you the most authentic happiness.

Secondly, allow that person to be whoever **they** are. Because fundamentally, THAT is the person you CHOSE to be with at an earlier stage in your relationship. So simply ALLOW them to be who they are. It is much tougher to change someone into being who you WANT them to be. And lastly, do all of this in the spirit of unconditional LOVE. Love is the overarching emotion that drives us all. Allowing love in all scenarios, and especially for yourself, will drive and direct all other emotions.

When in love, you allow. When you allow, you become more in tune with yourself in alignment. When you become more in tune with yourself, you increase your awareness (consciousness). When you increase your awareness, you tap into an abundance of bliss. In a state of true awareness and bliss, all desires are realized, including the emotions of love of yourself which translates into agape love for the one you're with. So when Tina Turner asks, "What's love got to do with it," you can answer love has EVERYTHING to do with it.

Chapter 22

'Take Good Care of Yourself'

"Be gentle with yourself. You are a child of the Universe, no less than the trees and the stars. In the noisy confusion of life, keep peace in your soul." — Max Ehrmann

Take good care of yourself...

This was something my mother said to me many, many times, particularly as we were about to leave one another or when we were saying goodbye on the phone. "Take good care of yourself, Edward." I can hear her words so clearly, poignant like a command of solace and warning. Usually, I would respond in my typical way of being nonchalant and coy, sort of shrugging it off, like 'okay, of course I will take care of myself, I already am taking good care of myself, what are you talking about?' is what I would be thinking.

What did she mean? I remember her expressing sincere concern for me, as she did often throughout my life. "You're doing too much. You need to slow down." I remember getting irritated and defensive, dismissing that wisdom in an I've-got-my-life-together sort of attitude.

After all, I worked out 4-5 days a week. I ate healthy meals. I drank at least 3 liters of water daily. I practiced Yoga several times a week. I spent time doing things I loved—movies, nice restaurants, exciting travel. And, on most nights I even slept a minimum of six hours. I had it together, right? Why slow down? If anything, I needed to speed it up, pick up the pace. If anything, I felt I was behind and needed to increase my efforts.

I took good care of myself—on the outside.

But on the inside, I buried vulnerability. I overcompensated for my insecurities. I used my wit and charm often to obtain things and manipulate people, particularly women. I played the resilience card. I was the king of quick fixes to remedy problems I encountered. And I was brilliant at convincing myself I was okay and that I had it all together.

I wasn't taking care of myself—emotionally.

I was taking good care of my outer world but was severely neglecting my inner world. Somewhere along the path of overachievement, chasing my goals, and trying to have it all, I lost the real meaning of good self-care or maybe I never really understood the meaning until now.

There was a movie I saw, *Southpaw,* where the main character, boxer Billy Hope, was in dire straits. His daughter had been taken away from him due to a careless loss of self-control, which cost him the life of his wife and eventually everything he'd worked so hard for. He was trying to return to the sport he'd been suspended from and loved so much in an attempt to regain custody of his daughter. In this pivotal point in the movie, Forrest Whitaker, who plays the boxer's new trainer, says to him, "...promise me one thing, that whatever happens, you will take care of yourself..."

Win, lose, or draw, he cautioned and commanded the boxer to take care of himself. The point was driven home that the outcome of the match was irrelevant, and that what was most important was that he care for himself—physically, emotionally, and spiritually.

So what have I come to understand my mother to mean all those years by 'take good care of yourself?' What action did I take after understanding what she meant?

I made a conscious and deliberate decision to be selfish. Not selfish in a grandiose, narcissistic type of way. I made the decision and purposeful intention to let how I feel be my number one priority. I started listening from within and following my eternal guidance system. I started deliberately focusing my thoughts, thinking on purpose and with purpose. I relinquished others of the responsibility of taking care of me and accepted full and complete responsibility of my own well-being.

THINK/WRITE/DO

1. Practice meditation and stillness every day.

2. Make it your daily intention to focus on the positive aspects of all that you see.

3. Travel distant places to connect instead of using it as an escape.

4. Purposely SLOW DOWN. Begin simplifying tasks and commit to DOING LESS, which, ironically, is when you will begin to achieve more.

5. Take time to breathe deeply and center yourself in stressful situations.

6. Learn to let go of the things you cannot control and understand that the ONLY thing you truly can control is how you choose to feel in any moment.

7. Let people and circumstances be exactly who and what they are.

8. Acknowledge your accomplishments and mini-successes and celebrate with small rewards instead of rushing to the next best thing.

9. Move away from a place of obligated action and more into an inspired action with the things you want to do.

10. Listen to your body more. Create sanctuaries—weekly time to relax and just be—instead of waiting for the crash and burn before replenishing.

11. Let go of disempowering beliefs that no longer serve you.

When you apply these things, suddenly, the world you've always lived in takes on a different appearance, a brighter and more abundant world with purpose and meaning. Your days become more joyous!

When we take the time to re-connect with ourselves, finding alignment with the God within, replace our fears with trust, and learn to let go of the things we cannot control…this is taking good care of ourselves.

When we listen to our intuition, embrace all of our imperfections, and stay authentic to who we are…this is taking good care of ourselves.

When we come out of the "Matrix" and focus our minds on what's REAL…this is taking good care of ourselves.

When we ground ourselves in the present and make mental space to find clarity…this is taking good care of ourselves.

When we learn to be gentle with ourselves, this is **truly** taking good care of ourselves.

How do YOU define taking good care of yourself from the inside out so that you can fully experience and have the best quality of life?

Chapter 23

Love as a Primary Emotion

"Love is a field of flowers filling the air with its gentle aroma as its petals dance in the wind and smile in the sunshine." – G Black

Love is the fundamental emotion that motivates life. From the time children are born, it is imperative for them to feel the touch of another human. That connection between mother and child is an outpouring of love that solidifies an eternal bond between the two. Falling in love with another person is also an experience that songwriters have attempted to explain through sultry lyrics and balladry since time began. It's the butterflies in the stomach, the fluttering of the heart, the joy and happiness just by the sound of the other person's voice. Love is gentle, compassionate, understanding, and non-judgmental. That's why it feels like sunshine and tastes like sweet rain. Since we come from a place of love and our God, our Creator, **is** love and we are created in His image, then love **must** be our primary emotion.

Imagine yourself in these various scenarios with those you love. Remember the birth of a child and the love you felt and still feel when you look at them. Reminisce on the innocent nervousness you felt when first falling in love with another. These are the feelings and emotions that tickle your soul. These feelings provide a platform for joy, happiness, and contentment. Love is a driver of life, forever looking to expand and share its lasting effects on all who experience it. Love is a catalyst to all that is ecstasy. So, given these facts…why do we ration our love as if it is scarce? Why do we hold it back as if we will run out of it? Why do we hold back a fundamental emotion that asks to be shared so it may be returned unto you?

How do we define who deserves the love we want to share? Do we base it on judgments dependent on the expected reciprocation of love from the other person? "I need to see if they will love ME before I can express love to THEM." Is this supposed to be some type of defense mechanism? What is it we are protecting? Our feelings, of course. We get it. But what about the **desired** feelings we have? Do we not desire to love and be loved? Do we not desire to create and experience joy and happiness? Are we too busy "protecting our feelings" to the point that we are restricting our possibilities? Restricting love stifles our desires of joy and happiness. The more we protect, safeguard, and ration love, the more fleeting love becomes in our lives.

Recently, I watched a story on television where a woman confronted the convicted murderer of her son. The woman showed incredible love and compassion toward the prisoner, telling him, "I forgive you for what you did to my son. And I love you in spite of your crimes." Frankly, I was shocked and at first overwhelmed with frustrated emotion as I tried to put myself in her shoes and thought about how I would feel in that situation. Later, I came to understand that this woman was opening her love to the man who killed her son, which allowed HER to regain joy, happiness, and contentment in her life. Without love and forgiveness, the woman would have remained in the bondage of her hatred, which stifles the emotions you truly desire. So for that, **it is important to understand the approach to ANYTHING and to ANYONE and to ANY SITUATION is through a sense of primary love.**

We oftentimes peddle or barter our love for others. This is a selfish way that only stifles our own growth. By giving love freely and willingly without the thought of outcome or consequence, we allow more love and light into our lives. Love is what we attract when we give it freely.

Approach your job with love in mind and watch your negative thoughts about Monday morning disappear. Approach your teenagers with love as a primary emotion and watch yourself start to understand where they are coming from, standing in the space they are standing. Approach your bills with love – yes your bills – understanding that you are grateful that you have means to create them and you expect to pay them.

Love is our home base. Love is what lifts spirits. Love should be given freely and frequently. It doesn't matter what happens on the other side of the equation. Simply lead with, approach, and offer **love** in all situations and circumstances. Period. What you will receive in return will astound you. All of your desires in life can be attained when operating from a fundamental basis of love.

Imagine...if you were a tree of love, your branches would be JOY, HAPPINESS, and PEACE, and your leaves would be SMILES, LAUGHTER, CONTENTMENT, and SUCCESS. By making love your primary emotion, we prune our tree of the stress, angst, frustration, and doubt we tend to feel. Our tree of love becomes more rooted as we replace those negative things with strength, confidence, and desired expectation. We remove fear and doubt, which allows the fruits of desire and expected outcomes to flourish. Our tree reaches for the sun with every confirmation, justification, and realized desire we experience. This is what happens when love operates as our primary emotion and not some scarce resource we look to protect.

Therefore, we invite you to wake up with love on your mind as your primary emotion. Approach any and all people and situations from the primary emotion of love. Pay attention to the responses you receive in return from people. Be attentive to how situations and circumstances start to unfold to your desires. Watch God's Universe and the order of things return to you that which you have given. The reciprocal of love is not based on another human. The reciprocal of love is based on God's law. Thus, it will be returned to you 100% of the time and without fail. Give it away. As much as possible. Give love away.

THINK/WRITE/DO

Did you take the time to imagine yourself as a tree of love? A tree whose branches are joy, happiness, peace, contentment, tranquility, etc. and whose leaves are smiles, laughter, and success? Imagine it. Now take the time to imagine how your branches stretch high and wide. Then imagine the people you encounter sitting at the base of your tree and enjoying the relaxing shade and protection of your existence. Feel the love that is shared.

As you go about your days, be the Tree of Love. Truly imagine yourself as this tree that is filled with love and seeks to share its love with all who encounter it. When you get to work, consciously look to your boss and coworkers with a sense of genuine love. Love them in your mind and watch how the love you have created branches out through your words and actions.

Approach all situations from a place of love primarily and take note, literally, of how those things, situations, circumstances and people respond. Love is a reciprocal activity. Love in some way, shape, or form will come back to you. Take a few days of practicing this. Journal the situation/circumstance and see what positive things happen. The more you practice this, the larger your Tree of Love will grow.

Chapter 24

The Potter or the Clay—Creation

There have been many sermons preached using the subject of the potter and the clay. In the Bible, the book of Jeremiah gives a depiction of this metaphor as do various other books in scripture. The process of pottery is a tedious and multi-step process that requires patience and diligence.

Pottery is made by forming a clay body into objects of a required shape and heating them to high temperatures in a kiln. This process removes all the water from the clay, inducing reactions that lead to permanent changes, including increasing the object's strength, and hardening and setting its shape. It requires a careful balance between water and dirt. Too much of one, not enough of the other and you cannot produce a sustainable product.

After the right amount of dirt and water is mixed, the right amounts of clay must be kneaded with the hands to incorporate or infuse the ingredients. The purpose of kneading is to remove air bubbles and to smooth out the grit within the clay. During the kneading process, the clay is handled roughly by the potter as she works out the impurities in it. At first the clay itself is abrasive and unresponsive but the more time the potter spends kneading it, the more elastic and pliable it becomes. It is interesting to note that the more resistance there is in the clay, the more apt it is to collapse during the process of molding. **In other words, for there to be a sustainable product, the clay must be free of any resistance.** Any "impurities" or "lumps" that interrupt the flow of smooth turning of the clay on the wheel and it will crumble OR produce an unwanted product.

There are other steps to this process, but the point is, it's not an overnight creation. It takes time, practice, patience, and concentrated focus.

Would you like instant manifestation in your life?

Do you think the potter, if possible, would choose to snap his fingers and BAM! Instant creation of the finished product? Would he, if given the power and opportunity, skip the creative process and go straight to the manifestation? And if so, what would be lost? What would be the cost of skipping the journey? I'm reminded of the TV sitcoms "Bewitched" and "I Dream of Jeannie" I watched as a child, where the main characters, with a twitch of the nose or blink of an eye, instantly could grant wishes and desires. Oftentimes their "masters" would not desire the instantaneous manifestations but rather wanted to go through the processes of attaining what they wanted.

If you had your very own personal genie, what would you instantly wish for? Millions of dollars? The vehicle of your dreams? Vacation homes? In our early stages of development, of course we desire material things like these mentioned, but as we grow and mature, we come to realize it's not the object that we desire, per se, but rather the feeling that we experience from acquiring the object. We think we would feel better in the attainment of the Rolls Royce or the acres of land, or the whatever. And certainly we do feel so good, so wonderful…for a little while, until the newness wears off or until we realize we want something else, etc. **It is the feeling we're searching for, not the material object!** No acquisition of anything or any person can ever give us what we're truly searching for.

So often we want our desires to manifest now. We want what we want and we want it to present itself instantly. But when we think about it, what kind of life would that be if all that we ever wanted we could instantly achieve? Think about that!

There is a process to creation for a reason. Whether it's the potter and the clay, the artist and his canvas, the song writer and her lyrics, or the chef standing before all his ingredients preparing for his masterpiece, it's the process one goes through in creating something out of nothing that ushers a magic, a certain power and force only demonstrated through concentrated focus. It's the process of creation that demonstrates God's power. Since we are created in His image, it is our fundamental desire to also create. But for us, **it's what you become along the journey towards the manifestation that's the most important. Who and what you become along the path is the reason for the path**!

My good friend took her entire summer and transformed her back patio into an oasis consisting of a water fall, beautiful greenery, a pond, and various other aesthetics. She created a very beautiful and tranquil space. She could have 'twitched her nose' and skipped the process by simply hiring a landscaping company to come and produce her idea and significantly shorten the journey to a quicker manifestation and enjoyment of what she wanted. But she chose to toil through every aspect of this creation, often running into major road blocks and hindrances that prolonged the process. It was both physically and mentally taxing. But her desire was greater than the obstacles that she faced. She understood that there was a force and power generated from the problems that she encountered that would not have been garnered without the problem. The problem CREATED a solution!

These are the creative forces God has given us. This force is manifested mainly through your journey towards creation. This is why we never really stop desiring to achieve and do things in our lives, all our lives. When we stop creating, we usually choose to leave this earth realm. **WE ARE BORN TO CREATE!** We all know innately we were put here for a reason. We were put here to do amazing things and achieve tremendous greatness!

Similar to the transformation of the caterpillar to a butterfly, the force isn't only a beautiful physical metamorphosis. It is creation at work. It requires a willingness to go through the process and the journey. Some caterpillars don't survive through the process to become butterflies.

Don't stagnate your growth and stifle your God-given potential by averting the process. Enjoy the journey along the path of creation. There is so much to gain in the process – alignment, joy, happiness, passion, contentment, bliss, etc. The question for you is…Are you the potter or the clay? Are you being the potter, living a life with deliberate intention to shape and mold your own destiny? Or are you the clay, being shaped and molded by your circumstances and situations?

Chapter 25

Empathy and Empowerment

Empathy – em·pa·thy ['empəTHē/]

noun – the ability to understand and share the feelings of another.

The San Bernardino attacks, 14 people killed. Treyvon Martin, a child shot to death. Eric Garner choked to death by police officers in New York. Sandy Hook Elementary School shooting in Connecticut, 20 children and 6 adults slain. The Paris Terror Attacks, 130 people killed. The Orlando killings, 50 people killed and 53 wounded.

These are chilling, terrifying events that are happening in our world today. The news and everywhere we turn bombards our lives with coverage of these atrocious events. As humans, we feel empathetic, sympathetic, horrified, troubled, sorrowed, angry, frustrated, unsafe, and victimized by the evil acts of others.

I am not immune to these feelings or thoughts that stem from empathy. I, too, feel concern, worry, anger, and compassion. "What is the world coming to? When will this stop? How can we keep our children safe? How do we thwart this evil?" These are some of the questions we tend to ask in response to what we see happening abroad and in our own communities. But before we become victimized by our own empathy, let us first understand empowerment.

Empowerment – em-pow-er-ment [ɪmˈpaʊəmənt]

noun –

1. The giving or delegation of power or authority; authorization
2. The giving of an ability; enablement or permission

Let us talk specifically to spiritual empowerment and what that means in our daily lives. First off, we are not human beings who occasionally have a spiritual experience. We are spiritual beings having a human experience. Everything about who you are begins with the understanding that you are a soul (ethereal being) manifesting yourself, your existence, through a body (material being). God, Allah, Jehovah, Source Power, The Creator, The Most High, created us in His image and has endowed us with the ability to CREATE, just as He has and continues to do in this material world. Therefore, when we consider spiritual empowerment, let us understand and be clear about the fact that The Creator has granted us the ability to alter, change, manifest, and create the realities we seek.

When considering evil and the evil acts that people or groups of people do, understand that evil is a distortion of a personal reality. **Evil is a distortion of a personal reality.** The young men from the Columbine High School massacre carried a distortion of their personal realities. It's not that they didn't actually feel picked on or bullied or depressed or left out, secluded, made fun of, etc., which is partly the reason why they did what they did. But more important to our understanding is those young men had a mutated sense of how to resolve what they felt and the distortion of their realities suggested they should kill to relieve the pain they felt by inflicting pain on others…hence, evil.

The same holds true for the various terrorist groups around the world and in our country. The same holds true for several law enforcement officers who carry out police brutality and senseless killings of innocent people. The same holds true for a mother who drowns her six children. All of these people have one thing in common – a distorted sense of a personal reality. However, we are empowered to facilitate and manifest change.

Let me offer one more idea and definition to complete this point: Groupthink.

Groupthink *is a psychological phenomenon that occurs within a group of people, in which the desire for harmony or conformity in the group results in an irrational or dysfunctional decision-making outcome. Group members try to minimize conflict and reach a consensus decision without critical evaluation of alternative viewpoints, by actively suppressing dissenting viewpoints, and by* <u>*isolating themselves from outside influences*</u>.

This could be any terrorist group, some groups of law enforcement, racist hate groups, etc. that perpetuate and act out the various heinous acts we see in our society today. So how do we combat or counteract this villainous behavior?

It begins with the empathy you feel. The empathy you feel screams, "This is wrong! This is unacceptable! This must STOP!" Where we miss the next step is by continuing to focus on what we perceive as "the problem" as opposed to focusing on the solution.

Our empathy takes over at times and we continue to wallow in the sorrow and the pain and the frustration and anger we feel toward the situation. This is where it is important to understand the Law of Attraction. <u>What you focus on expands.</u> The more we focus on what we feel regarding any given situation, it has no choice but to continue to grow and expand. Therefore, focusing on the solution is what will deliver your desired result.

As things happen in your life that make you uncomfortable, understand that in that very moment you are being given an opportunity to grow. You are being given a gift to expand and change for the better. It is up to us at that moment to choose…become a victim of our own empathy and continue to feel, think, and speak of the despair, destruction and pain; or choose to be spiritually empowered and devote our energies to the solutions of peace, harmony, synchronization, and unity. Either way, wherever we focus our energy, thought, feeling, and words…it will manifest. THIS is the spiritual empowerment the Creator has given to us as spiritual beings having a human experience.

So, imagine how Groupthink works for those people who are spiritually empowered and exercise that empowerment. One example of this is the Civil Rights Movement. Recently, I watched a series that Oprah Winfrey is heading up called *Super Soul Sessions* on the OWN Network. Of the shows I watched, everyone had a different perspective, with the common denominator being positivity and peace. When you consider Oprah Winfrey's platform or audience, no one can deny her reach. Millions of people are tuned into Oprah's broadcasts. So, when you organize an event where the sole purpose is to create and share more positivity and peace… Groupthink happens. But it happens in an ultra-positive way instead of the negative suppression of outside ideas or influences. With millions of people focusing on the solution as opposed to the perceived "problems," positivity snuffs out the evil that we spoke about. We all emit vibrational markers that are derived from what we think, feel and say. A collective vibrational marker based on peace, love, and harmony is the most powerful force in our Universe. Its power FAR outweighs the evil. Once again, evil is the distorted view of one's personal reality. So if we, the collective, decide that we desire peace and we set out to manifest that positive energy for peace and harmony, in search of manifesting solutions instead of focusing on perceived problems, then the positive outcomes and solutions have no choice but to show up in our lives. The Law of Attraction is absolute.

Stop to take a look at the various perceived challenges you have. Do not **focus** on them at all. Do not give power to your perceived lack of something. Instead, focus your energy and attention on what you desire. What is the reality you long for in your life? What is the reality you desire for our world? What is the reality you desire for your children? Those people who have a distorted sense of personal reality (evil) manifest their desires and outcomes. Do not think for one second that you don't have that same power to manifest your reality and the reality of others from a sense of positivity, harmony, and peace.

Use empathy as a catalyst for empowerment. If you're angry about terrorism, what is your desired outcome? And it shouldn't be to bomb the foreign country they came from. But instead, focus your energy on peaceful resolution and understanding for both sides. If you're frustrated with police brutality and seemingly reckless abandon for human life in America, focus your energies on a solution of safety and harmony between those police officers and the civilians of our country they protect. Again, use empathy as your catalyst for empowerment. God has given you the power to manifest the reality in which you desire.

The more people gain that understanding, the more peaceful the world will become and the happier you will be in your life despite the evil things you see happening in the world. A thunderstorm begins with one rain drop. Be that rain drop. The ocean is forever changed by the casting of a pebble. Be the pebble cast in the ocean that causes the ripple effect that alters the course of the current and waves. Be spiritually empowered.

Alignment

Alignment

One of the most liberating realizations in spiritual growth and development is understanding what it means to be in alignment from a spiritual and vibratory context.

The word "alignment" itself denotes a parallel relationship between two forces or objects. It's used to refer to many things in our world such as wheel alignments on your car, alignment in yoga postures, physical alignment or misalignment as it relates to the skeletal system, etc.

However, when we talk about alignment from the spiritual or vibratory context, we're talking about the most important alignment to consider, the 'granddaddy' of all alignments. It is the one indicator (via emotions) that reveals to you where you stand at any given point in time on any subject, in relationship to where your inner being stands on that same subject. More importantly, our ability to detect when we are out of alignment is one of the greatest gifts bestowed on us from the Creator.

Your inner being has a position and viewpoint on every single subject matter that you observe and/or partake in. What is it? What is the constant aligned position of the Creator? Love. Under the umbrella of love of course comes compassion, gratitude, joy, appreciation, understanding, etc. Positive emotion is the aligned position of the Creator. When we speak of spiritual alignment, we are talking about being aligned or in direct parallel relationship with positive, good feeling emotions. Our inner being's constant and consistent alignment is one of well-being. When we feel negative emotions such as fear, anger, resentment, bitterness, jealousy, envy, worry, etc., at that very moment we are misaligned or out of alignment with our inner being and our true selves. Negative emotion is the misaligned position we experience when we are assuming a position other than the one of our inner being. This does not mean that there is no necessity or great value in negative emotion. However, negative emotion is simply an indicator, and the best indicator to being out of alignment.

In the chapters ahead, we will explore and discuss spiritual alignment, how to get there and ways to most effectively get back in alignment when we fall out, as we invariably do. We will talk about the importance of preparing yourself early enough so that when things occur that have the potential to pull you away from your aligned position, you've already done the greatest part of the work towards realigning. We'll provide practical solutions you can apply to remove the speed bumps of life so you can consciously and deliberately choose the path that serves you best. We'll show you how to practically apply the use of spiritual alignment principles to create the life you truly desire, which employs spiritual empowerment. You will learn how to stay in alignment while navigating smoothly through trying circumstances and situations while others are falling apart.

Alignment and our ability to maintain that alignment is one, if not THE greatest, key to success. Likewise, our willingness to compromise and sacrifice our alignment is the greatest cause for our lack of success, unhappiness, illnesses, lack of fulfillment, and impediments to living a joyful life. Alignment is everything!

Chapter 26

Remove the Speed Bumps of Resistance

Imagine your mind as a car. Your life is the highway. You've set your destination and you start out on your journey. What stops you from reaching your destinations on life's joy ride? Speed limits slow you down. Potholes upset your ride. Fuel stops delay your arrival. And speed bumps throw you off course. These barriers impede your progress and sometimes derail your entire trip.

We all have desires in life. Desires are our proposed destinations. We have desires to achieve greater prosperity, better experiences, promotion, joy, love, etc. We unknowingly suppress our desires by creating the speed limits, pot holes, fuel stops, and speed bumps from our own thoughts, words, deeds, and actions. When we impart the perceived limitations of our resources, lack of knowledge or confidence, and embrace doubt, we create resistant barriers that keep us from reaching our destinations. So how do we remove these obstacles in an effort to make our journey smoother?

First, let's establish a few truths. God, Source, Allah, Jehovah, The Higher Power created the Universe and all the laws that govern it. Many of us tend to think we somehow operate outside of those laws set in place by God Who regulates this Universe. The sooner we can understand those laws, how our lives relate to those laws, and the power God has given us within this world working WITH those laws as opposed to outside of them, the smoother our journey will be. This doesn't mean your life is FREE of potholes and speed bumps. It simply means you develop a better way to navigate through and around those barriers.

Let's revisit one of the fundamental laws God put into place when creating the Universe — The Law of Attraction. The basic definition of LOA states that **energy attracts to itself other energy with which it's in *vibrational resonance.*** Therefore, if I believe I will set out to reach my destination without incident, I create an opportunity for achievement by emitting the energy that calls for unimpeded success. If I believe my journey will be difficult, I still create an opportunity, but the energy I emit calls for challenges and problems along the way. If I believe I will master great things in this life...I will. If I believe things will never go my way...they won't. This is how the Law of Attraction works. The Law of Attraction does not differentiate between positive and negative but rather on the vibrational marker that you produce.

So, for example, when you say, "I'd really love to get that promotion and I know I deserve it. But I know John has more experience than me," you just countered your own desire with the positive and then the negative. You just created your own pothole, speed bump or barrier, derailing yourself from reaching your destination.

Understand, the Law of Attraction is not simply wishing for the best or practicing positive thinking. Working the Law of Attraction is deliberate creation. We must envision ourselves in the place we desire.

When I prepare for a vacation to an island with my family, I envision the things we will do when we arrive there. I envision the white sands, smell of the ocean, and the beautiful palm trees. I see me lying in a hammock and hearing the waves of the ocean crashing on the beach. Then when we get there, that's exactly what happens as I have envisioned because we've been there before. So, I know what to expect. However, the same holds true for things we have not experienced before as well. Whatever your desire in this life, envision yourself in it, doing it, BEING it.

If it is the promotion on your job you seek, envision yourself doing the job, see yourself in the office, see the people reporting to you, see yourself handling business, being productive and efficient in that position. See yourself being recognized for the outstanding job you're doing in that position. See yourself receiving that large paycheck from doing the job.

Hold that vision without doubt, limits, or worry. Be confident in seeing yourself in that position.

The fundamental laws God has put into place are true and exact. The Earth is currently spinning at 1,036 miles per hour and will complete one full turn on its axis in exactly 23.93 hours. This is a fact. At the same time, there are nine other planets (including Pluto) that are all doing something similar. The point? The point is, everything operates in order. If you succumb to the order of things (ALIGNMENT) the way God has put them in place, including the Law of Attraction, your life can become more predictable. Resistance against those laws of order only stifle your journey.

THINK/WRITE/DO

Be a deliberate creator. Be in alignment with the authentic you, which is your soul. Be in alignment with what you truly desire. Hold the vision of what you desire and expect it to be manifested.

Relationships: Envision yourself in a healthy relationship full of all the things you desire in a mate. See yourself in various scenarios with that person doing the things that make you both happy.

Prosperity: Envision yourself being prosperous enjoying the material things you desire. See yourself driving that beautiful car you've wanted or sitting on your couch in the magnificent home you want.

Health: Envision yourself in wonderful health doing all the things you want to do in this physical body free of disease or affliction.

Whatever vibrational marker you hold, the more you envision it, WITHOUT the barriers of doubt, frustration, and angst, the quicker you will reach your desired destination on this life's journey. Remember the Law of Attraction — remove the speed bumps of resistance that come in the form of doubt, angst, and frustration. Hold and maintain the vibration of your desires with full expectation of receiving them. And simply...enjoy the ride of your life.

Chapter 27

The Path of Least Resistance

Many conversations have been discussed surrounding this subject of the **Path of Least Resistance (PoLR)**. Many of us take it to mean taking the easy way out of something, avoiding conflict, circumventing something challenging, etc. Some have proposed that the PoLR does not allow growth as it is from resistance that we expand and become stronger, e.g., muscle growth through weight lifting, commonly referred to as "resistance training." Likewise, life growth through trying experiences (resistance) can cause growth and expansion.

However, for the purposes of this discussion, we would like you to consider the PoLR as **the path of most allowing;** the path of clarity; the path of alignment. The PoLR in life is about vibration. Remember the Law of Attraction. In the vibrational realm of the Universe, attention to resistance attracts more resistance, which is completely contrary to the physical world where we have been taught to fight hard to overcome the resistance. We have been taught "no pain, no gain." We subscribe to going through some type of hardship in order to achieve success. This may be one way to achieve success, but it certainly is not the only way.

We are not encouraging fleeing from life's issues. We are suggesting taking the path of most allowing. One of the ways we align with our souls, the authentic you, is by taking note of how we feel. When considering the Path of Least Resistance, it is important to take note of how you feel first and then decide what you would like to feel next.

For example, I was traveling recently and had boarded an airplane. I was sitting in my favorite seat when I fly, the aisle seat. Soon a lady and her daughter boarded and were trying to figure out how to sit together, as they had been seated in separate seats. The daughter had a seat towards the front of the plane, in a middle seat (the seat I hate the most), and the mother had a seat right next to me, also in a middle seat. I sensed the mother trying to figure out if she would ask me to move or not. She politely asked if I would mind changing seats with her daughter. I did not answer right away. I told her to wait just one moment. So, here is one way we define taking the path of least resistance. I absolutely hate the middle seat. You might think that taking the PoLR would simply mean tell the lady, "Sorry ma'am. I'm extremely claustrophobic and cannot sit in the middle seat." But for me, to do that would not yield me the best feeling. I would be thinking about how I have separated a child from her mom. So, the path that offered the least amount of resistance for me was to give up my seat. I just needed a moment to line my energy up with that decision.

This same analogy can be applied to all aspects of your life when considering the Path of Least Resistance. The first step is to acknowledge what you feel and embrace that feeling without judgment. Second, simply allow. The situation is what the situation is for that moment. But more importantly, how are you defining that moment as it is happening? Put the moment or circumstance into perspective. And third, decide how you want to feel next. Do you WANT to be anxious, angry, frustrated, and irritated?

Taking the path of least resistance is more about exercising decisions that yield the greatest amount of allowance of happy feelings and joy (positive emotions), which is resistance-free. Sometimes, that may mean doing something that on the surface, you really don't want to do but that offers you the best path towards ultimate freedom, joy, and happiness.

You can tell you're in a state of resistance because you feel negative emotion about something. Feelings and emotions, as discussed in *The Eternal Guidance System (EGS),* are our eternal guidance system at work. Positive feelings indicate we're in the flow, which is "allowing." Negative feelings indicate we're blocking the flow, which is "resisting."

How do we take the path of least resistance when faced with a dilemma or when we're in a circumstance/situation that is causing stress?

THINK/WRITE/DO

Use the eternal guidance system you were born with. Be aware of your feelings and refuse to tolerate the negative emotions for long periods of time. This doesn't mean to ignore negative feelings. It means recognize them for what they are—indicators.

1. Acknowledge negative feelings first—because they are authentic indicators of something unwanted—and then:

    a. Clarify what it is you truly do want; decide how you want to feel. Then allow.

    b. If it's a circumstance beyond your control, turn the situation over to the Universe. If you have some measure of control over the circumstance, make a decision that yields you the best feeling; the decision that most aligns with your inner being. Then allow.

    c. Line your energy up with that decision, chill out, and allow yourself to feel good.

All that we have asked for and desire, God knows and has created the path to get to it; we just have to let go of resistance and allow the natural state of well-being to happen. Resistance comes in the form of doubt, anger, anxiety, frustration, and many other emotions and feelings we consider negative. Just as in *Removing the Speed Bumps of Resistance*, these emotions impede your progress. By taking the Path of Least Resistance, we realize a much smoother way. We feel relaxed and more at peace. We are not tossed and turned by the things happening around us while empowering ourselves to feel exactly how we choose to feel.

Chapter 28

The Answer Is You

Whatever the situation, whatever the problem or challenge you encounter, the answer is YOU! How many times do we look at the behaviors of others and say, "If this person or situation would be different, I would not be angry, or sad," or any of the other myriad of emotions we experience? We argue with our loved ones and then give them the responsibility to soothe us. We demand from our employers or employees that they conform to our desires so that we can feel good emotionally. We attempt to control our children in the name of keeping them safe and out of harm's way, and to lessen the aggravation we have within our own lives.

In reality, we are the answer to any problem we face—YOU and I. We cannot control the behaviors of others, or the outcome of certain situations. But what we **can** control is our ability to focus: Remember, **wherever we place our attention, especially with sustained focus, begins to manifest in our lives. Our choices of what we choose to focus on, and how we wish to respond to any given situation, will ultimately impact that very thing we wish to see change.**

It's truly about reclaiming your power through making decisions, getting in alignment, understanding perception, and vibration, etc. Knowing that you don't need anything or anyone to change in any given situation, but that you only need to change your own view or perception, is what creates the opportunity to take responsibility for our own well-being.

We all are inevitably faced with challenges. One primary solution is to become aware of our own ability to turn any and all situations around in our favor through our conscience and deliberate intention. We are able to hold ourselves accountable for the way we feel specific to our own moods and emotions. Turn inside. Look at what YOU can change about you to make the situation better. Mahatma Ghandi said it best: **"Be the change you wish to see."** You want to see humility and love in your mate, demonstrate it. You wish to see more respect from your children, give it. You want a society sensitive to overall humanity, live it. The solution to any problem lies within YOU and your choice of where you choose to focus your attention.

Chapter 29

Align for Your Best Stroke at Life

I'll never forget how elated I was when I shot the best golf game of my junior-amateur career some years back. I shot a spectacular 92! LOL... clearly, I wasn't planning on making any cuts or money on anybody's tournament, professional or otherwise. Nevertheless, it was a monumental victory for me at the time as I could count on one hand how many times I'd actually broken 100.

Golf is a sport that is positioned to challenge you both physically but more so mentally. THAT is the first lesson of golf. From an athletic perspective, I am more than fit in strength training, cardio, and overall fitness. But golf is really not about how much you can bench press or how fast you can run. None of that matters in golf. None of that plays any significant role whatsoever in terms of teeing off and getting the small white ball into the hole. It is more about your mind. More specifically, how is your mind aligned with your desired result?

Sometimes when I'm on the tee box, there's several people around and the thought comes to mind, "I'm going to KILL this shot! I'm going to launch this thing 300 yards. Just watch!" As I feel the testosterone course through my veins and my muscles tense up and prepare to strike with "God-given" force, I hit the ball. But instead of going 300 yards, it sputters just past the women's tees for about 75 yards instead. That's mainly because I'm trying to "muscle" the situation instead of aligning with my desires.

How many times a day do we look to "muscle" or control a situation in an effort to force it to succumb to our desired outcome? We don't let people into our lane in traffic as if we will get to our destination that much faster so we speed up and muscle them out. We bend the truth or embellish the facts to convince someone at work to vote our way on an issue. We ask someone to handle something and then take it completely over and do it ourselves for fear it won't turn out the way we want it to. We argue, debate, and defend our intellectual positions vehemently to prove we are "right." We "muscle" the situations we are faced with instead of allowing them to happen freely as they are designed to.

When I line up on the tee box, keep my head down, left arm straight, rotate my hips, and simply BREATHE and RELAX, I barely feel the ball when I strike it. It goes 300 yards (or something like that). Straight. Effortlessly. Releasing my perceived control allows my desired results to be realized. It is the difference between resisting and allowing. Resistance, also known as control, creates fear, anxiety, insecurity, frustration, worry, and anger. Allowing creates peace, calm, comfort, and contentment. Peace, calm, comfort, and contentment allow joy, happiness, freedom, and true love to come through.

Release your perceived need to control as we spoke about previously. The more we attempt to control, the less control we actually have. This goes back to the Law of Attraction. Ironic I know, but the fact is, when we attempt to control, we are attempting to avoid a non-desired result. The more we try to control in an effort to adjust to the result that we don't want, the more power the non-desired result gains. Why? Because we're focused on the non-desired result not happening. By simply expressing your desire, not doubting the outcome, and allowing it to happen, you can quickly realize your desires because you are in alignment with what you desire as opposed to being in alignment with your non-desired outcome. **The Law of Detachment** — express your heart-felt desire, envision its manifestation and immediately release it, detaching from the timing of when it will come. Release the need to control the outcomes of situations and circumstances.

One very important way to begin to release control is by releasing judgment. Release judgment starting with yourself. If I swing my golf club as hard as

I can because I'm trying to "kill the ball" and it only goes 50 feet, I need not judge myself on my swing and what I did wrong and beat myself up for making a bad shot. On the next shot, I simply need to start by expressing my desire to hit a good shot, breathe, relax, and simply allow it to happen, releasing the need to "impress" those around me. Release judgment of others as well.

Releasing judgment of others allows your mind to be free. When your mind is free, you make room for the allowing of creativity and manifestation. Judgment reflects a measurement of control. "If they do this then it means this." Or "I KNEW they would do that because that's what they always do." Or, "they always act like that. What do you expect?" The measurement of control is based on your perceptions, your fears, your anxieties, your frustrations, anger and/or insecurities. Releasing judgment of yourself and of others allows you to be open and free to create and allow your desired outcomes to be realized.

THINK/WRITE/DO

Align for your best stroke at life. Don't try to "muscle" your desires into existence. They don't like that. That's not the way the Universe works. Just like golf, it's not really about muscle, but more so about finesse. Align for your best stroke in life by doing the following:

1. Express your desires.
2. Write your visions.
3. Meditate on what your final outcomes look like.
4. Consciously envision your desires daily.
5. Release the need to control the absolute outcome.

Create. Manifest. Live. And simply be. Be one with yourself and you will live in your alignment. Living in your alignment will provide you with the best possible outcomes of the desires you have created. Don't muscle through. Just breathe. Relax. And swing.

Chapter 30

Align with What? And How?

Now that we've touched on some of the aspects of alignment, let's take a deeper dive into how to actually align and with what to align exactly. While we've spoken about alignment and being in alignment, you may have also heard others speak of this concept in other spaces. But what does being in alignment mean? We've heard others say that we need to be in alignment to create what we want. But what, exactly, does that mean? **What are we supposed to be in alignment with and how do we do it?**

We will assume you have arrived at understanding some basic concepts. That being, we are more nonphysical beings than physical. Yes, we obviously are both and we tend to get caught more in the physical world than the spiritual. But the fact of the matter is we are mostly spiritual beings—soul, ethereal, energy, vibrational, NONPHYSICAL. The larger part of us, our soul, is always in spirit. That inner part is connected to Source Energy or God. When we decide to experience the expansion of the physical world, we come into the physical body knowing we are always connected to that Source, that Higher Power.

Alignment with Who We Really Are

When we think of alignment, we can use the real-life analogy of wheel alignment. A wheel alignment on a vehicle essentially requires squaring wheels and axles with each other so that they're moving in the same direction. If you've ever experienced driving a vehicle that was out of alignment, you know how uncomfortable and potentially dangerous it can be. Your car fights against your efforts to stay straight. Your tires wear out quickly and unevenly. Isn't that interesting? Likewise, the alignment we seek, the squaring if you will, is with that larger part of ourselves—our soul, or source, which always loves.

When we experience something, we don't want, by way of feeling negative emotions about it, we automatically send out a desire/vibration/energy for the opposite. If we experience someone being disrespectful to us, we desire to be treated with respect. If we see the bills piling up and don't have enough money to cover them, let alone to do some of the things we want to do, we desire more money. If we are unhappy with our significant other, we want a better relationship. If we are unhappy and unfulfilled on our jobs or businesses, we want work that excites and fulfills us—and so on.

It is important to understand *this desire goes out as vibration whether we express it in words or not.* Our souls immediately expand into the new desire and become the vibrational equivalent of it. The Universe conspires to bring about that which you desire. The negative emotion of unhappiness, anger, fear, anxiousness, and frustration we feel is because we haven't caught up to the new version of ourselves at the soul level. We haven't caught up with the God level of our inner being.

So how do we catch up? How do we get into alignment with the new, expanded version of ourselves and see the manifestation of that in this physical reality?

We align by paying close attention to our feelings and making conscious and deliberate CHOICES that foster and promote our being happy and joyful. A previous chapter, *The Eternal Guidance System,* explained how we are all born with an internal guidance system called our emotions. Our emotions tell us when we are heading towards or away from what we want. Emotions communicate when we are in line with our higher being and when we are not. When we feel negative emotions such as fear, anger, resentment, worry, and so on, we are disconnecting ourselves from our Source and our well-being; we can become **out of alignment.** Likewise, when we feel hope, interest, positive expectation, happiness, joy, enthusiasm, appreciation, etc., we are allowing our flow and connection to

Source. **This is alignment**. How do we get in alignment? By intentionally seeking an emotional state that feels good and redirecting attention from that which does not.

Of course, when you are faced with situations that feel "insurmountable" and "terrible," it doesn't seem like an easy task to move in a direction of feeling good. We have long practiced the vibrations of fear and lack. It takes a concerted effort of will to decide to shift into a new way of thinking and feeling. But it can be done. And it works!

THINK/DO/WRITE

1. When you're put into a situation of stress or despair, find the **one** good thing in that situation and focus on it. Relish in being grateful for that **one thing** in a bad situation and you will begin to bring yourself back to the surface. Being in a good place attracts the best results. When things appear really bad, just lean in the direction of the next best feeling or thought.

For example: You just lost your job. You probably won't be able to jump immediately to alignment. Simply choose the closest thought you can think that makes you feel just a little bit better in that moment. Then choose the next thought that feels a little bit better, and the next, and so on. In a very short time you will feel better. You will notice yourself coming back into alignment.

If your perception of the situation or circumstance is that it's too bad to reach for a better feeling or thought, and despite your efforts you simply don't have what it takes right at that moment to think a better thought, then try engaging in some activity that you enjoy. Again, this takes effort on your part. The point is try everything possible to redirect your attention and focus until you feel better and then come back and address what needs to be addressed from a point of alignment.

2. Once you're in alignment and have practiced consistently enough to know what to do, begin to get a jump on keeping yourself aligned. Begin to consistently practice healthy ways to soothe yourself and

keep your energy on high levels no matter what you may perceive as "reality" at the time. Do this by engaging in activities that bring you the highest amounts of joy; e.g. yoga, weight training, jogging, walking, watching a funny movie, mediating, etc.

Here's a tip: The more your sensory system is involved in the activity of your choice, the higher frequency and vibration you will emit, and the more aligned with your inner being you will be.

Remember, however, alignment is more about controlling your thoughts and feelings. You can use physical activities to assist in bringing yourself back into alignment or use them to help stay there, but physical activities are only preceptors to your mental activity that must be performed. The physical activities simply make it easier to get mentally and vibrationally back to where you're trying to go.

Because whether you do it consciously or not, you are creating and manifesting realities all the time. If you're not conscious of what you're creating, you may create the experiences you don't want. Start from a place of alignment and begin new creations and new manifestations of the things you want. Practice consistently feeling better and purposefully keeping yourself in alignment with your higher self. You will gain access to solutions and ideas that once eluded you and will have an immediate impact on your life.

Chapter 31

Is Your Belief Serving or Limiting You?

What do you believe and is that belief serving you or limiting you?

There are constant conversations regarding beliefs. Some people fight and are willing to die for what they believe in. It's very interesting to hear what different people believe regarding various subjects, which sometimes challenge me to reassess my own personal beliefs to ensure that what I believe is not hindering my desires and are in alignment with my inner being.

It can be a frightening contemplation to realize you no longer believe something that you held true for years. It sometimes can destroy the very thing we've based our lives on. Some things we believe because it was what our parents believed and their parents before them. These beliefs are morays of society and/or cultures, etc., especially with regards to relationships, money, and religion. What's interesting is, we often continue our beliefs in spite of their obvious disempowerment, in spite of new experiences that our lives have taught us that provide support for new principles, and in spite of the fact that they simply just don't feel right.

Speaking of varying beliefs, I had a conversation with a friend whose belief, based on the Holy Bible's Genesis 3:16, was that she would always be in subordination of a man. The Bible verse states, *"To the woman he said, 'I will greatly increase your pains in childbearing; with pain you will give birth to children. Your desire will be for your husband, and he will rule over you.'"*

In another conversation, a friend expressed to me that no matter how much love her children showed their father regarding an estranged relationship, it was impossible to have any lasting effect. She based this on her own experience as a child growing up with her father.

In yet another conversation, it was expressed that despite any and all efforts made, a young lady believed it was next to impossible for her to have a good relationship with her brother. Both had broken each other's trust on multiple occasions.

The irony is they are all absolutely correct. The Universe, being a consistent deliverer, constantly reveals and supports every one of these scenarios. That's how it works—you believe something to be true then the Law of Attraction yields evidence to support that which you believe, and so the cycle goes on and on. This is why it is next to impossible to convince someone of anything other than what they believe to be true because they have "facts" to support that which they believe, whether it serves them well or hinders them. The true reality is YOU ARE THE CREATOR OF THE FACTS through your chronic thought patterns which equals beliefs.

A belief is a thought you've practiced long enough, over and over, until it becomes true for you. Some say limiting beliefs come from the subconscious. Others believe they come from our environment. Which came first, the belief or the life experience? It doesn't matter how we picked up limiting beliefs. The only thing that matters is that we recognize that the negative emotion we feel is pointing them out to us. Negative emotion is saying to us: You're holding a belief that is thwarting your light from shining. It's hindering the God force or creative life force that is naturally being drawn through you.

All personal breakthroughs begin with a change in beliefs. It is a change in the belief that you can do something. The moment we begin to honestly question our beliefs, and identify those that are limiting and the experiences we assign to them, we no longer feel absolutely certain about them. This opens the door to replacing our old, disempowering beliefs with new beliefs that support us in the direction we want to go. When we develop the absolute sense of certainty that powerful beliefs provide, then we can accomplish virtually anything our mind can conceive, including those things other people are certain are impossible.

Our belief is what gives us our compass for the direction in which we move. For many, many years, the majority of the world believed that the sun revolved around the Earth and not vice versa. And we can see how easy it was to believe that when you look out and it appears that the sun is rising and setting in the mornings and evenings. But it was first believed by one person and then the majority of humankind until a change in possibility was introduced. Now we know much more about not only Earth's rotation but several other planets and suns both in and out of our solar system.

Likewise, it wasn't until 1952 that anyone believed that it was even close to being possible that someone could run a mile in 4 minutes or less. Then came along Roger Bannister who ran the mile in 3 mins. 59.4 seconds. Shortly thereafter, many people broke the same record. A new "belief" had been created.

In a more recent example, Diana Nyad swam from Cuba to Florida in 2013. She swam 110 miles without the aid of shark deterrents. She completed this after five unsuccessful attempts, and at 64 years of age! It was one feat that many, if not all, believed impossible to do. The point here is, belief has a direct impact on the action or non-action taken as well as the desired or non-desired result.

Oftentimes, as we move through our day-to-day experience, we can tell when we have a limiting belief or if something is amiss within us. Being able to quickly identify when this is happening will aid in staying in alignment. The signs of us being out of alignment are the strong negative emotions that are within. It is important to understand that we create our own limiting beliefs, which pull us out of alignment. It often comes forthright after you have clearly identified something that you want. When you heighten the focus of some desire, the energy begins to move more quickly — the limiting energy becomes more evident. A basic example is the desire for financial independence, and then the almost simultaneous limiting belief that "it can't happen."

So, think about what you believe. What do you believe about yourself? What do you believe about your significant other? What do you believe about your financial circumstances? What do you believe about your friendships, your work your attitude, the world? What do you believe about everything? Identify your beliefs. Then ask yourself, "Is this belief serving me best towards attaining my true desires?" If they are not, here's a few things you can do:

Clearly identify the limiting belief. This requires some level of attention. The simplest approach usually is to look at what you're wanting in life, what your desires are, e.g., a better relationship with my estranged dad, a soul mate, more expendable income, etc. Then notice your beliefs regarding these desires.

*You might note how strong each belief is and what emotions they elicit in you. THIS IS USUALLY YOUR INDICATOR THAT THE BELIEF IS CONTRADICTORY TO WANT YOU WANT! Limiting beliefs usually contain the word "never," "can't," or "impossible," or contain absolutes like "always." You can count on a limiting belief to do one thing—NOT FEEL GOOD.

Acknowledge that these are beliefs, not truths! Realize that just because it's a belief you've carried around for a long time, doesn't mean it's true nor does it mean it can't change. This is often the hardest step.

"But, but, *my* limitations are *real*!" Here's the place where choice comes in. Which are you more interested in: defending your limitations to the death or achieving your goals and desires for life? Do you want to stick with the belief that, you now know for certain, is not serving you or adopt a new belief that yields you the results you want? As author Evelyn Waugh wrote, *"When we argue for our limitations, we get to keep them."* You choose.

Accept a different belief. There is nothing wrong with saying, "I no longer choose to believe that, I now believe this…" There is nothing noble about hanging onto a belief that disallows and disempowers you.

Use your imagination and try on a belief that is aligned with what you want. Make new and different statements that are no longer disempowering, and that support your new belief. The trick is to go beyond just saying it. You want to really step into this new belief and feel how it feels. Done thoroughly, this step and the one previous will go a long way toward dismantling your old limiting belief.

Take different action. WARNING: This might feel a little scary. After all, you've probably been practicing your belief for years. However, *act as if your new belief is true.*

In other words, if you really are a loving spouse, how would you act towards your husband/wife? What things would you do to demonstrate acts of love? If you really are capable and have learned a tremendous amount from past financial difficulties, what steps would you take now with the new belief that you can attain financial abundance? If you really are the kind of person who eats healthy food, what will you put in your grocery cart?

Sometimes new beliefs come naturally and require no effort whatsoever. Certain beliefs will no longer be applicable to your life experience and what you desire. They may simply no longer coincide with your Inner Being. And that is okay. You now know better, so as you evaluate your limiting beliefs, it becomes easier because the old belief no longer makes sense. More importantly, it doesn't feel right.

Chapter 32

Pay Me in Gratitude

God, our Creator, blessed each and every one of us when He granted us the power of imagination. Imagination is the catalyst for creation. Therefore, we have the power to change, alter, and create our reality at any given time. We have the authority to command our feelings within any given circumstance. Through imagination and creativity, we have the authentic influence on everything material. However, love and gratitude are what keeps us connected to God, Who allows and makes all of this possible. Authentic gratitude opens a flow of allowance that facilitates desire to be realized.

> *"Gratitude unlocks the fullness of life. It turns what we have into enough and more. It turns denial into acceptance, chaos to order, confusion to clarity. It can turn a meal into a feast. A house into a home. A stranger into a friend. Nothing around you changes. You change. When gratitude shifts the moment, it shifts you."* — *Melody Beatty*

Sometimes we lose sight of what's directly in front of us as we chase life's dreams and things. We continue to search for happiness in promotion and material possessions. This is one of the main reasons why our happiness eludes us or why our happiness is fleeting. Happiness does not exist in a thing or possession. Happiness exists within **us**. What are you grateful for that does not equate to a status symbol? Simple things such as the sunshine on your face, the laughter of a child, affection from a loved one; these things cannot be purchased or achieved. They simply are. Just as our authentic being just IS.

When we are in search of our authentic selves, we discover that our true being is continuously grateful. Our authentic being is ethereal. Therefore, nothing material will ever truly satisfy it. Our true being is beyond material things. Material things are manifested by our true being. They go from imagination to creation. However, the gratitude we find in things that are <u>not material,</u> are the things that satisfy our souls. Sometimes we become callous to what truly satisfies as we redefine who we think we are by the things we possess.

Recently, I've heard tons of catch phrases, such as, "I'm leaning in" or "Be in the moment." These are very powerful statements and can change your life and your reality if truly implemented.

A while ago, two co-workers walked into my office and I was extremely busy. Honestly, I didn't want to talk and they showed up to chit chat. I CHOSE to "lean in and be in the moment" even though I did not want to because I was focused on my work. What I thought would have been a short "water-cooler" talk of about 10 mins. turned into an hour-long enlightening discussion. What was supposed to be about the simplicity of the day and insignificant banter turned into a deeper spiritual conversation about alignment and enlightenment. What was supposed to be an interruption of my day turned into a spiritual flow of fellowship. When the conversations were complete, the co-workers thanked me. But I was the one truly thank FULL.

Finding and spending time with those types of moments are what we should live for. The truly authentic moments in life are what symbolize and reflect true value for our souls. Those experiences are what tickle our souls and provide the **wealth** our souls need to be rich. Authentic experiences are the currency our authentic beings covet. What is most interesting is we have opportunities for those moments on a daily basis if we simply pay attention. Pay attention to the moment and not what you expect out of it.

Through meditation, I embrace gratitude. The energy, excitement, and overall joy and happiness found there cannot be recreated from anything that I own. Again, the energy, excitement, and overall joy and happiness found there cannot be recreated from anything that I own. It cannot be provided by any other person in my life. It is always there waiting for me to acknowledge it and in return NEVER fails to provide delight and pleasure.

Stop what you are doing and close your eyes. Focus on three things you are truly grateful for that can't be purchased. Focus on those three things and why you are grateful for them. Seriously…do that now.

Spend time in this moment. Be in this moment. Lean into this moment of gratitude. Linger in the emotion of gratitude you feel about the three things you are focused on. Is it hard NOT to smile? Is it hard NOT to feel joy and contentment within this moment? Is it hard NOT to see your circumstances in a brighter light? YES! You feel like smiling, being joyous and content, and your life shows you a brighter perspective. Why? Because now you have touched on your soul's joy button. And it responds in kind. Gratitude changes life. Gratitude changes perspective. Gratitude creates authentic reality. Gratitude fosters grace.

Continue to focus your attention on what you are grateful for that cannot be bought and paid for.

THINK/WRITE/DO

Gratitude changes your perspective and alters your reality to be more aligned with your soul. The beauty of it all is there is a formula we can apply to guarantee sustained happiness in our lives. Simply contemplate the following:

-We are vibrational beings.
  o The Universe responds to our vibrational markers and delivers back to us the same.
    ▪ Therefore, if I continue to express gratitude in the things of non-material,
      • which then lightens my soul and brings me joy because I am grateful,
        o which mitigates my resistance amid my circumstances because I am expressing gratitude,

- thus, creating a true sense of allowing,
  - then all my desires are free to flow effortlessly to me!

Read that again and know **"gratitude unlocks the fullness of life."**

Chapter 33

Alignment—The Midas Touch

The story of King Midas is from Greek mythology. It shows us what happens when true happiness, wealth, and abundance go unappreciated. This is the opposite of gratitude. Midas was a king of great fortune who ruled his country in Asia Minor. He possessed everything a king could desire—servants, a life of leisure, and complete luxury. He shared his abundant life with his daughter and staff. Although King Midas was very rich, he found his greatest happiness in the acquisition of gold. His avarice was so profound that he would spend many hours of his day consumed with counting gold coins he'd acquired and basking in the desire to obtain more gold. It became his obsession.

One day, Midas was presented with Silenus, a man who'd been found in the King's gardens passed out from drunkenness. He reeked of foul odor and was ungodly in his appearance. While all the King's staff wanted nothing to do with Silenus, Midas showed great compassion for him, showering him with kindness, generosity, and hospitality.

For his kindness, Midas was granted any wish he desired; whatever he wanted he would be given. Midas wished, "That everything I touch turn to gold." His wish was granted. He went around his palace, touching various objects, all of which turned immediately into gold. HE WAS IN HEAVEN! Or so he thought.

He sat at the table to have breakfast and took a rose between his hands to smell its fragrance. When he touched it, the rose became gold. "I will have to absorb the fragrance without touching the roses, I suppose," he thought in disappointment. Without even thinking, he ate a grape, but it also turned into gold. The same happened with a slice of bread and a glass of water. Suddenly, he started to sense fear. He could no longer enjoy the "simple" pleasures of life. But he had his gold.

As tears filled his eyes, his beloved daughter entered the room. When Midas hugged her, she turned into a golden statue! Midas was overcome with panic and sadness. In a desperate attempt to regain his previous life, Midas petitioned the god who had granted him the wish, turned curse, to be removed from him. Midas' life was returned back to what it was with his beloved daughter, newfound joy, and his increased appreciation and gratitude for all his life was.

How often do we wish we had the Midas touch? How often do we see celebrities and entertainers living lavish lifestyles and it appears they have the "Midas touch?" It looks from the outside that everything they touch turns into gold, but do we lose sight and not realize or appreciate the abundance of wealth we already possess? Isn't it interesting that we want the very things that we perceive we can't have? 'Someone is always living a better life' it seems, or 'I don't have enough. I need that or this to make my life complete.'

King Midas felt he did not have enough gold. He was already rich, possessing enormous amounts of wealth beyond measure. He was a king, for crying out loud! He lived a king's lifestyle. But, **more importantly,** he possessed the wealth and abundance of love!

The story is basically about how the giving away of your treasures and loving unconditionally will bring you to your **true and authentic** heart's desires. Midas had unconditional love for his family and all his servants. They did not consider themselves to be servants but rather part of his family. Midas demonstrated his unconditional love even for one considered to be the worst of the worst, a beggar, a bum of sorts; someone who none would normally associate with. Midas welcomed this person into his home. He clothed him, fed him, and had him cleaned up. Even though he was a king, Midas was giving of all that he possessed to those who were less fortunate than he. And once he truly understood what was truly important other than creating gold, he fell into full and complete alignment with who and what he was. For his willingness to unconditionally give his love, what happened? HE WAS GRANTED HIS HEART'S DESIRES! Even though his original desires may have come from a place of greed, a sense of lack, and an inability to appreciate what he presently had, because he gave of himself, his time, and his riches to another, he was granted his authentic desires.

All we ever really need to do to have all that we want is to, first and foremost, be grateful for what we have and appreciate the wealth we already possess. THIS CAN NOT BE UNDERSTATED! There are so many things to be grateful for. The way to attain more or to attain what you don't have is to appreciate what you have now!

Of course, this may sound like foolishness. "My bank account is zero. I'm living paycheck to paycheck, and you want me to be grateful?" YES! And if you really want to manifest your desires, try giving away some of what you feel you already don't have enough of. You don't have enough time in your day? Find a way to give more of it away to something you consider noble and worthwhile. And watch more 'time' come back to you. You don't have enough money? Give away some of the little you already don't have. Believe me there is someone in worse shape than you! YOU most certainly need your 100 to 1000 thousand dollars like nobody's business. But I bet it would not be a hard task to find someone who needs it more than you do. If you do this freely and out of love, material and money will come flowing back to you. It is the **Law of Reciprocity**.

We only use time and money as examples as they are most often the two commodities people THINK they need more of. Being unattached and giving freely of what you have, even if you think it is not enough, brings to your life more of what you want just like King Midas. But the key is to not be consumed and/or become a slave to your desires. But you can do that too if you so choose.

Chapter 34

What if…

"What if you could be anything, or anybody, you chose to be? Think about it. What would you choose to be?" — *Nido Qubein*

What if you awakened in the morning and felt the best feeling you'd ever felt? What if, for some strange reason, you had this extraordinary feeling of well-being? What if you felt a feeling of invincibility; a feeling of enormous clarity; a feeling of being sure-footed, supreme confidence, a knowing that any decision you made on this day would be the very best decision EVER. What if you woke up one morning and just knew in your heart of hearts that nothing, no *thing* could shatter the joy you felt? That come what may, you just knew you would be fine and that you could thrive under any and all conditions this world handed you! What if you woke up one morning feeling independent and free? Free and independent of the need of any and all circumstances of life to be anything but as they are. What if you didn't need any person in your life to do or **be** anything other than who they were? Not your husband, wife, girlfriend, boyfriend—nobody? How empowering would you feel? And how would this empowerment impact other areas of your life? What if you woke up one morning and you just felt GOOD, full of joy and contentment?!

What if…you decided to live life without fear?

Then imagine you left your residence still feeling this overwhelming sense of peace and serenity. What if you went to work, school or wherever you needed to go and everything that could possibly go right, went right! You had nothing but great interaction with every single person you came in contact with. What if today was the day you went for that big promotion at your job? What if today was the day you took the big leap and started your own business or blog or website? What if today was the day you decided to leave that unhealthy relationship that you've been wanting to get out of? What if this was your day, full of nothing but greatness and positive outcomes from start to finish. You make it back home at the end of the day and think to yourself, I OWNED THIS DAY! This was the best day ever!

We all wonder what could have been and what could be. But how we think about the "what ifs" of our lives can have a huge impact on the ways in which we actually live.

Isn't it interesting how negative thoughts come into play almost immediately behind any type of plain ol' run-of-the-mill, ordinary situation? Missed a phone call from the mechanic—what if they tell me I need a brand-new transmission? Funny sensation in my arm—what if I'm having a heart attack? My boss wants to see me—what if he decides they no longer need me?

Even the most positive people among us run into negative thinking and negative thought patterns that must be dealt with. We've been somewhat conditioned to expect the best but also plan or be prepared for the worst, which subconsciously means expecting the worst. It's like in the back of our minds we know we don't deserve or can't truly fathom the best outcomes from our lives. We can't expect the best, and **only** the best ALL THE TIME! Nobody can do that, right? Wrong.

Remember this formula: BELIEF + EXPECATION = YOUR POINT OF ATTRACTION. You believe it. You expect it. It must be manifested. If you want to immediately improve your energy and boost your level of creativity, stop assuming the worst about things that haven't happened yet.

To get yourself out of this habit, you can start by transitioning from negative thoughts to positive thoughts simply by using the word "or." For example, "What if I need a new transmission? OR what if they're just calling to say, 'It's going to take a little longer than expected to complete the repair?'" Another example, "What if my boss wants to fire me? OR what if my boss wants to offer me a new position? Or compliment me on the good job I'm doing?" The point is, stop jumping to the worst-case scenario and choose the best-case scenario.

Using "or" to quickly counter a negative thought with a positive thought gets you offering a new and different vibration while reprogramming your thoughts when contemplating the future. **Eventually, you'll be able to skip the negative thoughts altogether and assume the best.**

Use your imagination to your greatest benefit/advantage, not your greatest liability. You have absolutely nothing to lose and everything to gain. People say, "Why get my hopes up?" Answer: WHEN YOU GET YOUR HOPES UP, YOUR LIFE GOES UP! It's your expectation/hope/belief/faith in yourself that is either hindering you or catapulting you to your highest points. Get your hopes up and keep them up! If you get your hopes up and it doesn't turn out the way you want, rest assured that **you**, at minimum, raised your vibrational frequency and that continued practice of this will yield the outcomes you desire.

Use your "what ifs" to dream big and to deliberately create your future. Remember, you get what you think about. What you spend the most mental time focusing on, either deliberately or undeliberate, is generally what translates into your life experience.

Using the "what ifs" towards dreaming the big dream forces us to use our imagination. Imagination is one of, if not **the** most important, key element in creation. **Imagination is the power of God.** It is God demonstrating His power through you! It's been said many times, "If you can conceive it, you can achieve it."

This world tends to shun dreamers. "Stop dreaming and come back into reality," they say. But what we are saying to you is, dreamers *are* the reality creators. We are the ones who, through our imagination and focused attention, create worlds. We want you to know that YOU have the power not to simply face reality but rather summon the power of Source, the power of God to create the "reality" that YOU desire for yourself.

What if this was true? All things would be possible. What if you decided to simply try and make the conscious and deliberate intention to "what if" yourself a new and different outcome? A new and different life of limitless possibilities? Is there anything to lose? What if…you win?

THINK/WRITE/DO

Make this a game. Don't be attached to the outcome. Simply have fun with your imagination.

1. **Make a list of all the best scenarios you can imagine. In other words, "what if everything you ever desired, dreamed about, yearned for… happened."**

   • What would you do?
   • Would you be able to receive all this good with open arms?
   • Who would you become?
   • Who would you help first?

2. **We recommend journaling your feelings and observations. Reflect on what you learned about yourself that you now have leverage for who and what you desire to be, do, or have.**

   • What if I could be whoever I wanted to be? Who would I be?
   • What if I could do whatever I wanted to do today? What would I do?
   • What if I could have whatever I wanted? What would I ask for?

Stretch your imagination as far as you possibly can for this part. Ask yourself the "what if question," and then visualize what that looks and feels like. You're dreaming, so there are no boundaries. Go for it. Dream big. The Universe knows no difference between what we call big and small. When you ask 'what if' and the answer comes by imagining, envisioning and feeling, you are asking and summoning the Universe and all its power to deliver to you that which you are asking for and answering. SO, BE PREPARED! J

3. **Put your "what if" into action. You can also use the "what if game" to make changes in your life with things that cause you challenges.**

For example: It could be that you get very angry when people disagree with you, or the fact that you don't eat as nutritionally as you'd like, or that you can't motivate yourself to write that novel because what if… I fail?

Whatever it is, notice it and be honest that it's YOU that's actually creating the problem by way of your inaction or your reaction, and your idea of the perceived outcome.

- What if I just sat down and wrote a page of my novel?
- What if I let go of my need to be right, and let that other person believe what they want to believe?
- What if I just go out and walk for 15 minutes and then decide whether or not I want to play the "what if" game about exercising again tomorrow.

Just to see what might come of changing the way you behave or perceive for a little while by playing the game.

4. **Have no attachments to the outcome**—Just notice what happens. But have zero attachments to the outcome. If the outcomes were positive, great! If they were less than expected, no big deal, try again tomorrow. THERE ARE NO LOSERS TO THIS GAME! Experiment with the same What If again until it just becomes your new way of being.

5. **Don't give up on your What-If's**—You cannot develop muscle without repetition. So, be prepared to play the game consistently for a time. We suggest 30 days at best.

When you get used to asking What If in the positive direction, you'll start noticing that your reactions to situations are easier, more in alignment, and open to SO many more possibilities. What if… you just try it for 30 days?

Chapter 35

Find Peace in Meditation

"True consciousness resides in the gap between thoughts." — *Deepak Chopra*

In the hustle and bustle of our everyday lives, nothing provides a sweeter comfort sometimes than simple silence. However, the silencing of our minds is much easier said than done for many of us. We are perpetually multi-tasking — feeding the dog while contemplating dinner for the family while answering text messages, with the television on in the background because there's a new episode of "something" on, while still thinking about the presentation you have to give at work tomorrow...all at the same time. Then we leverage technology, which is supposed to make our lives "easier," but it provides even more distraction away from our **true** selves as we hide behind likes and re-tweets in social media to determine our happiness and worth.

Recently, I went to a restaurant for dinner where there was a 20-minute wait. I looked around at the other people waiting and counted 13. The 13 people, ranging from 8 years old to 80 years old, were ALL face down with a cell phone. All of them. These are the types of distractions that keep us living at life's 'surface.'

Meditation provides a break in "the noise" of everyday life. It's "the noise" that oftentimes generates false realities, fabricated boundaries, and self-inflicted limits on our lives. In the silence is where we find authenticity and truth. In the silence is where we find meaning and purpose for our lives. In the silence is where we find clarity. Deepak Chopra has described consciousness as a rushing river. I will attempt to paraphrase his message:

At the river's surface, there is a ton of commotion. The rapids are tumultuous and the river churns and twists and turns. It is very noisy as it rages along. About midway of the river's surface the current is still strong. But it is less noisy. It moves with distinct purpose and the flow is steady yet calmer than the surface. At the bottom of the river there is absolute stillness. The sediment at the bottom does not move unless disturbed. Things are very still. Very calm. It is very quiet.

Our consciousness operates the same. Our everyday lives are the river's surface. Work, kids, bills, traffic, soccer games, grocery stores, arguments, meetings, presentations, reality television, cell phones, etc. These are the noisy distractions of what we call 'everyday life.' Many of us live strictly on the surface 100% of the time, ignoring what lies beneath. These are our everyday **perceptions**, which we tend to mistake for authentic reality.

Our **minds** reside at the middle depth of the river...analyzing, contemplating, making decisions on what we 'see' at the surface. This can become a sort of 'mental trap' when our perceptions become our realities. Our minds attempt to depend on what we see to interpret what is "real."

Our **souls**, our authentic being, the REAL you lives at the bottom of the river and watches in silence as an observer. This is the quiet space of the authentic you not burdened, ruffled, or moved by what is happening on "the surface" of your life. THIS is the place we go during meditation. This is where you find authenticity because this is the space where one truly fellowships with one's self. The core of your being...the core of your soul.

"You don't have a soul. You ARE a soul. You have a body." — C.S. Lewis

In the next section, we will talk about where your desires are born and how to manifest them. But it is important to note, it all starts with communing with who you truly are. Meditation is a great place to begin to do just that.

In the midst of the perceived chaos that surrounds you, there is comfort, safety, and confidence at the core of your being. Why? Because your soul is the keeper of all that is true to you. Spending time, at the "bottom of the river" in meditation puts everything that happens at the surface of the river, "everyday life," into perspective and provides clarity and understanding. It is the place where all questions and answers are clear because they are your own. They are the questions and answers that are right for YOU.

It is the place where you become a co-creator with God to express your desires and create an atmosphere where those desires can be safely planted and cultivated to grow, unimpeded by falsehoods from the surface that stifle due to doubt, fear, and anxiety created by your **perceptions**. At the bottom of the river lies the fertile ground where infinite possibilities for your life's purpose and desires are simply waiting for your focus and attention.

Your soul has no limits. No boundaries. No labels. Just potential and possibility. Spending time with yourself, your soul, will provide direction, clarity, and the spontaneous fulfillment of your desires. It is from this place that God communicates. So how do we quiet our minds long enough to get to the bottom of the river?

THIINK/WRITE/DO

There are many ways people meditate or work to get to that space of meditation. We provided one meditation activity earlier. Here is another meditation technique that may be helpful:

1. The first thing is to find a place that is comfortable and quiet. Set up a place where you will not be disturbed and set a timer on your distracting cell phone for however long you want to meditate. To begin, 10-15 minutes is long enough.

2. Breathe. Take note of your breathing. Relax and just breathe in and out slowly and deliberately.

3. Imagine yourself sitting on the banks of a very still lake. The meadow around you is fresh with the air of Spring. There are large

oak trees surrounding you and there's a gentle breeze blowing across your face. The lake is very calm and very still. You continue to take in the beauty that surrounds you and you feel a sense of peace, calm and contentment.

4. As thoughts try to come into your mind, turn them into snowflakes that descend upon the lake and dissipate on the surface without causing one single ripple in the water. Any and every thought is turned into a snowflake that falls upon the lake.

5. As the snowflakes continue to dissipate, soon there are no more snowflakes that fall and you are left with the silence of your soul. You may feel the anxious need to do something, think something, act on something, because this is not the space you're used to. You've been accustomed and conditioned to distraction. It is here where you want to hold your resolve and continue to commune in the space of silence. Simply relax. Simply be.

Practicing this technique of relaxation to meditation will open doors of peace, calm, clarity, confidence, and direction. It is truly operating from the inside out as opposed to the outside in. Meaning, instead of you **being directed** by your current circumstances or situations, you **become director** of your circumstances and situations. You become the author of your life, creating chapters for others to read as opposed to being the reader of the chapters and reacting to them as if you had nothing to do with their creation.

Your eyes see. Your mind interprets and provides meaning. Your soul is the filter that clarifies, screens, and provides authentic truths to the meanings you have perceived. However, we oftentimes get stuck on the first two without going deeper in our understanding. That is equivalent to living on the surface of our rivers of life; being tossed around, churned upside down and all around by the rapids and currents of everyday life.

Understanding that FIRST you are a soul with a body as opposed to being first a body with a soul will provide clarity to your authentic being. It will reveal who you TRULY are. Meditating is an effective way to spend time with the real you to provide real meaning as opposed to deriving meaning from those things outside of your soul or outside of the real you.

Put the cell phones down. Turn the television off. Single-task instead of multi-task. The world will not stop when you do this. Spend some time in silence with yourself. Your soul has been dying to join in the conversation of your life. Stop ignoring it. Consider your dependence on what your eyes see and what your mind interprets. Then let your soul provide clarity, meaning, purpose, and direction. After all, it knows what it's talking about because it is the real you.

Chapter 36

The Exercise

The longer we continue down the road of enlightenment, the more we practice alignment, the more we learn about and understand Universal Laws, the more we come to realize that it is a continual practice, an **exercise**.

Although LOA is unerringly consistent and is the basis for which we have or have not that which we desire, IT TAKES PRACTICE! It is an exercise of the mind. You are training your mind or, in most cases, re-training your mind to think the thoughts that you want it to think. This is one of the biggest secrets, which, once applied, will have immediate effects on your life. One of the most profound realizations for me was understanding that I could control the thoughts I had; that just because I had a thought didn't mean I was powerless over choosing the next thought, and the next thought, and so on. I came to realize the more I "exercised" this ability, two things happened: one, I got better and better at it, and two I began to see EVIDENCE of how my new ability was affecting my life and those around me in a most positive way.

I also found it interesting that, believe it or not, LOA is working at all times. You do not have to believe it for it to work for you or against you. The key is learning how to harness and leverage the power to maximize these principles to your advantage. We've discussed at length the power of belief and how belief basically trumps everything. What you believe to be true about any particular thing usually and generally yields more evidence of that thing. And certainly this is true. This is LOA at work with both your passive beliefs as well as your most passionate desires. IT JUST WORKS! Sort of like gravity and electricity. Whether we believe it or not, they both are always at work and can be immediately tried and tested for results, both positive and negative, that will support what you believe.

So, what do we know regarding LOA? What we focus on expands. What we give our attention to grows and we get more things like that to give our attention to. Focus on feeling better for 30-60 seconds, and notice how you gain access to thoughts that feel even better. Focus on something for a whole day and notice yourself having unlimited thoughts and evidence that support that topic. Pick a subject and give your full attention for an entire week and you will FEEL that topic resonating in your spirit, in your heart and mind. Focus your undivided attention on something for a month and watch how it manifests in your life in various ways. The proof is always in the changes you see and feel. The challenges are breaking the tendencies of careless, lazy, and/or limiting thoughts, and where we choose to devote our attention. We ignore our emotions, which are ALWAYS our best indicator regarding our alignment, or lack thereof, and where we should be devoting our energies.

If you can exercise your ability, which you can, to focus your undivided attention on something you desire somewhere between 30 seconds to 30 days, depending on your own level of resistance, you will see progress and evidence towards your desire. What happens most times is that we have a desire, we follow the steps towards achieving it, and when it doesn't manifest quick enough from whatever time allowance we've put on it, we lose momentum and traction and eventually start to go back to those negative patterns of thinking regarding the subject.

So, the question remains…what's the missing link? Visualization and imagination. You believe something, you expect it. Now, can you clearly visualize and imagine yourself doing, being, and having that which you desire? And if you can see it, how long can you sustain this visualization in your mind? Can you feel the feeling of having the desire without having the desire? But wait, how can I feel like I have something that I don't have? This is the exercise!

If you can conjure up the feeling from your power of imagination, LOA will deliver it to you in real-life manifestation as quickly or as long as your resistance allows it. But here's the key. When you focus your attention somewhere, you usually have an accompanied feeling or emotion about it. This feeling alerts the Universe to give you more of that thing you are resonating with, whether you actually want it or not. By giving your attention to something, you are CHOOSING it. This is an inclusion, attraction-based Universe, and there are no exclusions. When you say and feel YES to something, you trigger a response from the Universe. When you say NO to something, you're also triggering a response from the Universe that says give me more of this, even if you don't want it. So, people ask how did I attract this unwanted thing/situation into my life? By giving your attention to the essence of the subject. **The Universe is responding to you. What are you responding to?**

So, if you have a desire, but every time you offer thoughts about your desire, you feel bad for not having it or for the lack of it, you keep that desire away from you longer. The exercise is doing all that is necessary to instead feel the joy of the desire right now!

Take the example of money. If you've decided you would like more money, then your first step would be to identify your current beliefs on money. What do you say to yourself when thinking on the topic of money? Well, obviously, anything you're wanting more of, you're noticing the lack of. And usually it's the lack of or the 'not enough of something' where our attention and energy flows. If you've been desiring and trying for a while to increase your income with no change in your condition, then you will undoubtedly have some contradictory vibrational signals you are offering that the Universe is responding to. Sometimes we will feel optimistic and other times we may feel like it is an impossibility. We may feel inadequate, devalued, less than, frustrated, angry, or even sadness around our current financial situations. LOA responds to all of this. You will find yourself in a "one step forward, two steps back" cycle with a continued focus on the perceived inadequacies or perceived lack. In this cycle, it will seem like nothing is changing, when in fact it IS changing—constantly. It's just changing to more of the same. When you catch yourself in this cycle, just recognize it for what it is; a thought that can be changed of your own volition. They are simply practiced thoughts that you have control over. You can begin to practice new and different thoughts that better align with your desired emotions and desired outcomes.

The secret, the exercise, your goal is to reach for a thought and a feeling about money that feels true, that you can visualize in your mind's eye, but that also allows Law of Attraction to work in your favor. This provides you the greatest advantage towards manifestation.

The thought of "I am a millionaire" may be too much of a stretch (you'll know by how you feel when you visualize it). But the thought, "I am meeting my needs right now with my current finances and I am eagerly anticipating more money in the future" might be a truer statement for you right now that doesn't offer much resistance. Remember you can feel resistance. And if you feel some resistance in the thought, reach for another one. Find the thought you love in this moment that you can smile about! Eventually you will find thoughts that offer very little to no resistance, that feel true AND that reinforce the reality of the condition you are seeking. It's feeling good <u>right now</u> that matters. Practicing and learning how to stay in that good feeling place on ANY given topic is the exercise.

Chapter 37

The Power of Appreciation

We thank you for taking time out of your busy schedule to read what we believe is inspiring yet pragmatic information. We are appreciative. Every year, many Americans take at least one day to reflect and offer gratitude and appreciation; that's usually during the Thanksgiving holiday. But let us remember, not as cliché, but as a way of life, that every day should be a day of thanksgiving or giving thanks. Therefore, we are truly grateful to you today for spending time to read this book.

Giving thanks—Gratitude—Appreciation

Gratitude or, better yet, appreciation (there is a difference) is arguably the most effective, yet the most underutilized, unrealized influence that has the power to affect sustained positive change. "An attitude of gratitude." We've heard it, read it, and some have even experienced it. But how does keeping an "attitude of gratitude" or staying in appreciation affect our lives so powerfully? What do these forces have to do with us achieving our desires?

The simple answer is when we appreciate what we have, the Law of Attraction gives us more to appreciate. And likewise, when we are ungrateful, we emit vibrations that impede the flow of the things we desire. Law of Attraction states "that which is like unto itself is drawn." Like attracts like. What we focus on, expands. These are the ways the Law of Attraction works. So, having a sincere feeling of appreciation and sustaining it opens the doors for us to receive more things to appreciate.

Thanksgiving/Appreciation: One of the most under-utilized powers of the Universe

How it works.

When we appreciate something, we almost always experience some emotion or feeling. For example: If you take a moment to appreciate the time spent with your family or a loved one during the holidays, you will sense and feel some emotion. You're going to feel good about this because you're focusing on the positive aspects of the family or loved one. These feelings or emotions that you utilize when you appreciate someone or something will attract more positive things and more positive people into your life. THIS IS A FEELING-BASED UNIVERSE! It's all about how you feel and the vibration you are emitting at any given point.

Why it works.

Whatever we focus on, we will attract. Whatever emotions we attach to what we focus on, we attract in greater quantity.

This is why it is so important to be mindful of what we place our thoughts on. Thoughts generate one level of emotion. Speaking on what we're thinking about generates greater levels of emotion. And finally, acting on what we've been thinking about generates an even higher level of emotion. Therefore, we encourage you to THINK and SPEAK only on those things you desire. This is certainly an 'exercise!'

This Law of Appreciation is one of the Universal Laws that God has put into place for us to live the best lives we can. If we focus on something positive, we will attract more positive situations. If we focus on something negative, we will attract more negative situations.

The results of Appreciation/Gratitude/Thanksgiving start working for you the minute you start appreciating the things that you have in life. Try it and watch the emotional shift you enjoy.

THINK/WRITE/DO

Take a moment to appreciate something in your life. RIGHT NOW! It can be anything. You can appreciate the meal you had at breakfast, lunch, or dinner, or a conversation you had with a friend, your ability to read these words—anything. **Hint:** It is usually best to keep it general. Sometimes the more specific you get the more you find something to complain about.

When you do that, your mind shifts, your focus shifts, your emotions shift, and the energy you send out shifts. Instead of focusing on something negative and attracting more negative situations, you start feeling better and you start attracting more positive situations into your life.

We know what some of you will say—"The reality is that sometimes there are not a lot of great things to appreciate. Sure, I could find something, but I still have to find a way to pay the bills and get out of this rut that I am in." And to that we say, yes, you do. But here's the best part—when you work with the Law of Appreciation, you will attract the situations that you want to improve your life. The Universe will do the work it's designed to do in co-creating with you those things you've asked for and that you are in vibrational harmony with. Guaranteed. It's really that simple.

Now that you understand how appreciation and thanksgiving work, and how they can dramatically improve the quality of your life, try the following for the next consecutive 30 days.

- Every day when you wake up in the morning, before you even get out of bed, take a moment, it doesn't have to be long, and just appreciate. Remember, stay general. Appreciate your bed, the softness of your pillow and sheets, the comfort of the space you're in. Appreciate the new day that you have. It's a chance to start fresh, make a difference, have a positive impact on someone, share your generosity, or perform a kind act. This is a fresh start—a day that will never happen again! Say to yourself: "This is the very first day to the rest of my life." Approach it with eagerness and zeal! As you get out of bed and begin to get ready, continue your appreciation, keeping it simple and basic. Appreciate all that you see. Stay general and try hard not to think of today's events or to-do's.

- As the day goes on—After you've been consumed with work for a few hours, usually at about lunch time is a good time to do this next exercise. Find something that has already taken place during the day or the day before that you can appreciate. Simply find one thing that you really appreciate. It can be anything, small or large. It doesn't matter. Just fill yourself up with that feeling of appreciation about that one thing.

- At the end of your day—Preferably in the early evening, perhaps on your way home from work, take a few moments to appreciate the people you encountered on this day. New people, usual people, doesn't matter, even those who you really don't like or care for. **It is a blessing to co-create with others throughout the day and everybody plays a role in your movie!** This process allows you to continue enjoying their presence in your life while at the same time attracting more, positive people into your experience.

- Finally, as you go to bed at night — I have found this to be the second most important part of the process (second only to the morning process). Simply appreciate all the wonderful things that happened during the day. Don't limit yourself to appreciating only the big things that took place. Appreciate the little things that happened during the day. You didn't have traffic issues, you got a parking space close to the door, or maybe you just felt really good most if not all of the day. Sometimes you may feel your day was overwhelming and you may even call it a bad day. Really, there are no bad days, just bad ways of looking at things that happened during the day. If you still feel that you truly had a bad day, at least you got through it and survived. That's something you can appreciate.

Live your life in a state of thanksgiving for just 30 days and watch it have a profound impact on your experience. Give thanks, appreciate, and be grateful.

Chapter 38

Getting Comfortable in the Uncomfortable

I have been a Bikram Yoga student for a few years. For those of you who aren't sure what that is, Bikram Yoga consists of 26 yoga poses, carried out for two sets about 20-30 seconds per posture over a period of 90 minutes in a room heated to around 105 degrees (or hotter at times). It has been THE most challenging thing I have ever consistently done and made a practiced way of living. If you know me, then you know that I DON'T LIKE BEING HOT! Lying on a beach under the sun has a certain appeal, but I'm one of those people who can only fall asleep with the air conditioning on a cold setting or with the ceiling fan on even in the winter. So, needless to say, any type of hot yoga is contradictory to what's reasonable and sensible to me.

Yoga itself can be challenging enough. There is the breath control, the stillness, the quieting of the mind, the flexibility and balance, all of which are contrary to our ordinary, everyday lives, and require discipline and patience. Bikram Yoga, however, takes it a little bit further, in that it adds the heat factor. Now, imagine being in a room this hot with anywhere from 10-20 other people in the room and there's someone commanding you to bend over backwards and touch the floor! Put your hands under your heels, but don't bend your legs. Stand on one leg while simultaneously kicking the other leg out in front of you and place your head on your knee. Oh, by the way, don't forget to breathe slowly in/out through your nose only. And by the way, "we know it's hot in here, but keep going." At this moment you're thinking, "This is caaaraaazy!" But the funny thing is, the more you practice, the more you find yourself **getting comfortable in the uncomfortable.**

And here's where the lesson comes in carries over into my everyday life. See, what I have found to be true is that I can find joy in what appears to be an uncomfortable situation. I learned that I can find peace and serenity in a very uncomfortable circumstance. I can find happiness and contentment in what's perceivably the most unbearable event. **I am learning to live unconditionally!** I am not allowing conditions to dictate my happiness agenda; not allowing what's happening in my outside world to negatively affect my inside world. Living unconditionally, I am caring more about my inner well-being than what's going on around me. It means staying centered and grounded when everything close to me is saying, "Respond to me, and respond to me now." I've also learned from Bikram Yoga that you never 'master' the pose. You simply continue to hone your skill and technique. This is why I am "learning" to live unconditionally.

This Bikram Yoga practice has taught me that it's not really about the temperature in the room or the discomfort at the bottom of my right leg. It's not about the backed-up traffic or the rude person I encountered at the store. It's not even about the life-changing news that came to me today. But it's about finding a way to **get comfortable in the uncomfortable.** Finding a way to separate the present condition from the way I feel even if the present condition is significantly impacting the way I feel. Oh, it is truly an 'exercise' for living!

Getting comfortable in the uncomfortable doesn't mean putting up with or tolerating that which you don't want. It's not compromise or sacrifice. It's not learning to like something or living with something you really don't like. That would be offering resistance. It means using the power of your thoughts to allow the path of least resistance from where you currently stand towards where you want to be (even if where I want to be sometimes is out of the hot ass room). It means coming into understanding that circumstances don't really mean diddly-squat! They are just that, usually short periods of time of something occurring, which is something else about yoga that I use in my everyday life. The postures are generally 20-30 seconds, which means in my mind, no matter how uncomfortable

I am, it soon will be over. This is as it is in life, granted I sometimes don't have the luxury of knowing the time frame of the circumstance and when something I'm experiencing will come to an end as in Bikram. But I know that it will be over at some point and until that point comes, I will use the power of my thoughts to change and alter the vibration of the circumstance, thus making the circumstance null and powerless over me.

Remember: Circumstances don't MATTER, only your state of being MATTERS. "State of being materializes your experience, therefore choose the state of being you prefer, and then redefine the circumstance from that state of being."— *Chapter 4, Circumstances Don't Matter*

Challenges can be painful, extremely uncomfortable, taxing on the mind, body, AND spirit. But it's important to remember that they don't last forever. **Every painful situation has an ending!** In Bikram, there are certain poses that can be pretty agonizing for the body. During that pose, it feels as though it will never end. Your mind tells you, "Get out of here and get out now!" Sweat is trickling down your forehead, eyes are burning, muscles are screaming, sometimes sweat flies on to your body from the person next to you; sometimes I just know at any second I'm about to pass out!

But then suddenly, just as I think my body can't take any more, the pose is over. And guess what? My muscles recover. I feel fine. *I survived it.* More than surviving it, I now have a new basis from which I will practice life— from the "I can do this" basis; from the "nothing is as bad as it seems" basis; from the "all is well" basis. What a wonderful life lesson!

The take away: Conditions are rarely ideal in life. Would you really and truly want that any way? The deal is, stop trying to find the perfect conditions in order to feel the way you want to feel. Use the power of your thoughts to create the conditions you prefer. Use your own God-given power to change the condition to what you want it to be. It never gets much cooler in the yoga room, and it never gets a whole lot easier, but it is me that is getting better and better! Find YOUR comfort in the uncomfortable.

THINK/WRITE/DO

The next time you're in a comfortable circumstance, here are five ways to find comfort in the midst of your discomfort:

1. Know for certain that whatever the situation is, **it will not last forever.**

2. **Breathe through it.** Stop, become aware of how you feel, take several long deep breaths, then proceed.

3. **Clear your head**—Every time you are in an uncomfortable situation, your inner voice gets really loud. The only way to make it quiet is to clear the noise on the outside and inside of you. A little meditation goes a long way in providing space and calm to both your head and soul.

4. **Push yourself past your comfort zone**—Whatever the situation is, at some point, you are going to say to yourself, "This is too hard" or "I don't know what I'm doing." Here's a trick: Don't say it out loud. Just pretend to be confident. Fake it 'till you make it. It may be scary, but I promise you this: When it's over, you are going to say, "It wasn't as bad as I thought it was."

5. **Envision yourself on the other side of the situation.** See yourself already having gone through the uncomfortable situation. See yourself with a big smile on your face.

Remember: You have the same Source of energy flowing through you that creates nations and worlds. There isn't much on this Earth that you cannot handle.

Enlightenment

Enlightenment

Enlightenment. The perceived 'mecca of the mind.' That place that is elusive to most. That place that is only achieved after living in the mountains in a temple for 50 years. That ambiguous place of the mind only understood by the mystics of ancient times. Yeah…that's not what enlightenment is all about. But these are some of the things we've been led to believe.

PLEASE DO NOT MISUNDERSTAND, there is nothing wrong with any of that. However, a simple understanding of enlightenment is living every day with sustained awareness of authentic reality. That still may sound ambiguous or confusing. Not to worry, we will explore enlightenment in depth during this section. However, there are a few things that help us along our road to sustaining awareness on an authentic level. Spending time in meditation, prayer, silence, stillness, or even on top of a mountain in a temple for 50 years, most definitely helps to mold and shape our authentic understanding of reality. But the point is, enlightenment should not be viewed as elusive or difficult to achieve. Enlightenment is for us all and can be achieved by all. Enlightenment is about being aware. Fully aware.

Enlightenment is not a destination. It is more so a journey. Along that journey, we become more and more aware of what is real and what is created and accepted as real. Enlightenment is like a long road trip with various stops of recognition along the way, with each stop revealing more about YOU than the previous stop.

Along the road of enlightenment, we learn the role of our ego is not to be the truth teller but to be the storyteller. Or, better said, the teller of stories, stories that become truths in our minds. Enlightenment provides an awareness that allows us to 'see' the stories and 'see' the authentic truth at the same time.

Enlightenment also allows us ***to recognize and see the beauty of ALL things.*** It gives us the ability to see the beauty and value in all circumstances, situations, relationships, and occurrences. Enlightenment is recognizing that all situations, circumstances, people, objects, etc., operate as instruments in the symphony of life. Enlightenment is a heightened or elevated state of conscious awareness that things are the way they are. And that YOU—and you alone—have creative control over your life. With an understanding of enlightenment, or better yet a self-realization of your own enlightenment, comes liberation. An enlightened mind is a free mind.

Just as it's more nourishing and delightful to eat an apple rather than read about one, so it can be more rewarding to explore the movements of your own awareness and enlightenment than to try to understand this notion mentally. While definitions of enlightenment can be helpful, it can also be beneficial to not have too many characterizations where we attempt to fit our conscious awareness into a box, which could interfere with our actual experience. Maybe the best definition of enlightenment is no definition at all. Then, there would only be what is found in your own direct experience of consciousness and awareness.

Let's take a journey on the road to enlightenment in the next chapters to help discover ways to identify what is authentically true in your life by becoming more aware.

Chapter 39

Decision Making Made Easy

"When someone makes a decision, he is really diving into a strong current that will carry him to places he had never dreamed of when he first made the decision." — Paul Coelho, The Alchemist

"Every decision you make—every decision—is not a decision about what to DO. It's a decision about Who You ARE. It is the purpose of your soul to announce and to declare, to be and to express, to experience and to fulfill Who You Really Are." — Neale Donald Walsch

It has been stated that we make, on average, about 35,000 decisions in a day. On the surface, that seems like a lot of decision making, but obviously, it stands to reason when we think about all the choices we make from the smallest to the largest. Of course, this number may vary depending on your line of work, chosen professions, life's calling, etc. We decide whether to get out bed or not, how to pursue our endeavors, who to spend our lives with, what to eat, where to eat and so on.

If you're like me, you've probably been taught that decisions are critical, that every significant and crucial decision you make can have everlasting effects on your life from that point forward. While it is certainly true that some decisions we make do have consequences that can change the course of our lives, how we choose to view these consequences is up to us. But we should first understand that the decisions we make are not necessarily life sentences. We may view them as having a negative or a positive impact.

But the thing that I've learned is that it is not about the decision we make. It is that we make a decision. Just DECIDE! What happens when we consciously decide on something? When we make a decision and then line up with that decision, we summon the powers of the Universe to assist us in bringing that choice into fruition. We garner forces that would otherwise lie dormant and we allow ourselves to become a conduit for the God Force to express power. WE ALLOW GOD TO DEMONSTRATE POWER THROUGH US! This would otherwise not happen were it not for our intentional and conscious decision making. This is also why a little turmoil is good for us because often we won't make a tough decision until we're in a tough situation. Conflict and turmoil provide focus for our desires and intentions. In the middle of these challenges, we make a decision and things move very quickly to affirm our decision. Why? How? It is the Life Force that we have suddenly called forth.

The Universe is always conspiring to bring about our desires when we, first of all, know what we want and, secondly, make the decision to be in alignment with that choice. This is why it is so important to simply CHOOSE. Make a choice, then line up with that choice. Don't decide and then spend energy living in regret and second guessing yourself. This only diminishes the power you have just ushered into your being. Even if you must change your mind on a decision already made, it still serves you better than sitting around stewing and regretting a decision you made. Don't put so much pressure on yourself to make the "perfectly right" decision. The power of creation cannot EVER be activated within an indecisive mind. Therefore, focus your mind to bring yourself out of "mental limbo." The worse that could happen is that the consequence causes expansion/growth and new desire. Of course this may be a little oversimplified in that, obviously, some decisions are vastly more important than others. But the point is, the more we get into the habit of intentional and deliberate decision making, the easier it becomes in making "harder" choices. This is part of becoming Deliberate Creators and creating our own realities. God has endowed all of us with the freedom to choose, the freedom to make our own choices in life. Exercise it! And watch the power you are able to harness.

Chapter 40

Change or Transformation?

The word **change** is defined by Webster's Dictionary as "to make the form, nature, content, future course, etc., of [something] different from what it is or from what it would be if left alone." You change your hairstyle. You change your socks. You change your mind.

The word **transformation** takes "changing" to another level. Transformation is defined by Webster's Dictionary as "changing from one form, appearance, structure, character or type to another." Caterpillars to butterflies. Planted seeds to edible crops. Sperm and egg to human beings. None of these things are possible without transformation.

If you take hydrogen and oxygen in two separate containers on one shelf and put them on opposite sides of the room, then you've changed their location. The hydrogen and oxygen are dry, gaseous, invisible elements. The change that was made was in the location of the containers, not what was inside of the containers. Change. If we combined the two of them, two parts hydrogen and one part oxygen, they would form H_2O, also known as water. What was once dry, gaseous, and invisible now becomes wet, non-gaseous, and tangible water. The hydrogen and oxygen have now been transformed. The elements are still present, just transformed.

Change, while valid and valued, almost implies something superficial or temporary. Transformation implies depth and something permanent.

Oftentimes, we seek "change" in our society to correct the tribulations and miseries of our times. Currently, we have much civil unrest in America: racism, classism, separatism, political dissention, religious discord, the list goes on. We march and rally for change expecting that change will fix these things. We search for leaders to 'show us the way' to pull us out of some perceived darkness. We vote. We make our voices heard. After all, this is America and we will not be denied our inalienable rights.

But the real power of change lies in transformation.

Contemplate transformation. We must first start with our perception. I heard someone say, "Perception is reality." That person is 100% correct, but perhaps not in the way that we historically have thought about this quip. Our perception is what we create. When many begin to agree on the same perception, it becomes a reality. When many begin to accept the things that they agree they are seeing as reality, it becomes a truth. When many accept what they feel is truth, it becomes a belief. The belief solidifies the perceived reality that one person began.

Now consider transformation again and I will provide an example. A very good friend of mine, whom I trust completely, went to an event. During the event, the group she was listening to set up a fire pit of burning coals. The speaker told people that they would be able to walk across the burning coals in their bare feet without being burned. My friend did that and she was not burned or harmed in any way. I'm sure you have either seen or heard of this happening before, right? So, what magic, hocus-pocus, mumbo jumbo are they using to make that happen? Remember, our perception is what we create. So I perceive the coals are hot, but I also perceive that my feet can take the heat and be just fine. I agree with myself that what I perceive is my reality. My reality is, I have the ability to walk on fiery hot coals. I accept the reality I have created, therefore it becomes truth. I accept the truth of what I've just done and it becomes my belief.

Now let's flip the coin. What beliefs are you currently carrying that are simple distortions of your perception? Think about the stereotypes you carry. What about the judgments you pass? And what of the habits you maintain all in the name of "well this is just who I am." Or, "it is what it is." Is it? Or is it who you perceive yourself to be which has become your reality which has become your truth which has become your belief. "Perception is reality" and "Well, this is just who I am. It is what it is" are cop-outs to creation. In the example given, my friend CREATED an environment wherein she perceived, made it reality, made it truth, and believed she could, would and did walk on fiery coals without incident. Creation is the catalyst for transformation. God has given us all that innate ability to create.

Don't be satisfied with whatever judgments you have levied upon yourself. You have the ability to transform yourself to be whatever and whomever you decide. Not one situation on Earth has power over what is first perceived and then believed. You simply need to begin to change your perception. Change your pattern of thought. Change your mental alignment.

God resides in all things. To that end, in the Holy Bible, Paul references in Romans 12:2, "Do not conform any longer to the pattern of this world, but be **transformed** by the renewing of your mind." For me, I have "transformed." I have transformed because my perception, reality, truth, and beliefs are not prisoners to what someone else has determined to be authentic. So I choose to share with YOU that the same fear, anger, hatred, and depression that feed terrorism, racism, separatism, classism, social unrest, and discord only have the power that you ALLOW them to have.

If you recall the Law of Attraction—energy attracts to itself other energy with which it's in *vibrational resonance*—then you begin to understand you have the ability to transform any given situation, emotion, perception, or belief. Change your mental alignment for transformed change. Begin with meditation for increased awareness and consciousness of self. Once your understanding of self grows, begin to create the reality you desire by modifying "realities" you or others have created. Why should you be broke because Mama was broke? The wealth you create for yourself should not begin with a job. It should begin with the wealth you value within yourself. This goes for all things. Material, emotional, mental, and spiritual—ALL things. Create the reality you desire and transform your being.

Exercise your power of creation and start walking on your own fiery hot coals without incident. Don't look for change in **people** to change the world. The change you seek in the world begins with a transformation within yourself. The transformation within yourself begins with your perception of what you consider to be real.

THINK/WRITE/DO

Don't be a "Cop-Out-Creator." Are you the person who says, "It is what it is?" Or do you say, "This is just who I am…period?" Is that what you truly believe? Or is that a simple distortion of perception and reality? Are you copping out on your creative prowess? Truth is, we have power over those perceptions. Let's exercise that power.

1. Aside from your religious belief, identify one belief that is absolute to you. These beliefs are usually identifiable when we think of them and use words such as always and never. e.g. my boss is always a jerk, Linda only cares about herself, my ex will never change. What one belief is absolute to you?

2. Whatever you have identified, write it down and offer three counterpoints to your current belief. e.g. Linda only cares about herself—Linda is a great mom, Linda loves her family, Linda helped me when I was in need one time.

3. Going forward, be absolute with your counterpoints instead of the point you started with. So, in other words, think of Linda as a great mom who loves her family and remember the one time when she helped you in your time of need.

When we offer an alternative perception to something we are absolute about, we begin to create transformation through our creation of a new reality. And remember, energy attracts to itself other energy with which it's in *vibrational resonance*—then you begin to understand you have the ability to transform any given situation, emotion, perception, or belief. You will begin to see Linda in a completely different light and that which you offer Linda through your perception will be returned to you. A new reality.

Chapter 41

Living From the Inside Out vs. the Outside In

We are all guilty of being caught up in today's rat race—working to pay bills, traffic jams, reality shows, and hustle and bustle. We are all caught up in what we see in the news and are affected by what we consider to be the ills and injustices of the world. We tend to follow the frustrations of our stress and the things around us we allow to stress us. We live from the outside in as opposed to the inside out. Meaning, we watch and participate in the things happening around us in the outside world, interpret them, and let them direct how we feel to define our current reality, as opposed to the opposite. The opposite would be us creating within ourselves the expectations of our reality and then watching it unfold before our eyes. Admittedly, it is tough to wrap our heads around terrorism, high crime rates, and what seems to be a continuous loop of police crime. How on Earth do we live in a world such as ours and not be affected by what we see? By remembering WE are made in God's image. Therefore, we should live from the inside out, not the outside in.

In a previous chapter, we spoke about the fact that we are the "cutting edge of thought." This means that we are the cutting edge of creation. Creation begins with thought. Thought manifests through word and word manifests through actions. Actions create new realities.

There are many debates as to how this Universe and our world were created. But for the purposes of this discussion, our belief is that God is the creator of all that we are and all that we know. To that end, in the beginning, God spoke light into existence and the void was filled. Everything was created because He SPOKE it into existence. Understand, those things that are intangible create and control the tangible. The spiritual and the ethereal dominate all that is perceived. Therefore, there is absolute power in thought and word. In addition, there is only allowance and resistance. Therefore, the "evil" of the world we see is simply a manifestation of resistance. Resistance of the mind shows itself apparent in fear, anger, hatred, worry, despair, terror, and judgment. It plays out in actions that are qualified as "evil." It is only defeated by allowance, not more resistance. Allowance manifests itself in love first and foremost, and is followed by joy, happiness, contentment, absence of judgment, and peace.

I was shocked when I read an excerpt from Mahatma Gandhi where he spoke about the impending Nazi threats to invade and steal all the valued treasures, riches, and relics throughout Europe. His response was, "Let them come and **allow** them to take what they will." I never understood Dr. Martin Luther King Jr.'s position of non-violence and peaceful protest marches despite the police dog attacks, being spat upon, and being beaten. But he allowed it to happen that way. I was always baffled as a child in Sunday School class where my teacher taught all about the power of Jesus and His decision not to ever express that power against those who persecuted Him. He **allowed** it to happen. To be clear, the act of "allowing" does not mean you sit back and let another person violate you, your space, or your property. As stated, the act of allowing offers a vehicle for desires to be realized. All three of the people mentioned never wavered from their desires. So as things continued to happen that were contrary to their desires, they never abandoned their focus. The art of allowing means you don't go into a situation forcing or muscling your desired outcome. In the emotionally charged events we experience, our emotions should provide directions, but not the road map.

I've lost count of the number of police officer-related beatings, shootings, and killings that have taken place in our country over the years. We can all debate whether these actions are justified or not. And retaliatory violence solves nothing. As we discussed in Chapter 14, *Us vs. Them*, we all play the role of an "us" or a "them" in most situations until we learn, there is only an "us." Either way, the unrest between law enforcement and civilians seems to continue to happen. These things have sparked an enormous amount of righteous anger, seemingly justified in our society, especially within the African-American and Latino communities since these acts of violence seemingly have happened disproportionately to people of color. Within those communities, the frustration and the anger comes from a feeling of helplessness against the brutality and inhumane police atrocities that seem to go unpunished in a prejudicial one-sided judicial system set up to protect its own. **THIS** is living and having an understanding from the outside in. **To "fix" this situation and stop the perpetuity of it all, we must live and have an understanding from the inside out.**

The authentic truth is we are made in God's image. He has given us power and dominion within this world. This world is made of physical things and physical acts, but we are ethereal beings. We have lost sight of this understanding and therefore live from the outside in. God has given us both the power and the authority to manifest thought Ý to word Ý to action Ý to reality. Allowance is not weakness. Allowance is the vehicle that provides a way for our desires to be realized. THIS is why people like Gandhi, King, and Jesus were able to make strides in history in the midst of perceived chaos. We have been given the power and the authority to create what it is that we desire. But first understand we come from a place of love, which is also a place of allowance. Love does not live in a state of resistance. So, that which we desire, if we expect it to be created, must also come from a place of love, not hate, and not from a mental place of retaliation or righteous anger.

First, there is no judgment as to how a person feels. Feeling what you feel is personal to YOU and there is no judgment in that. The key is interpreting what you feel and knowing how to manage that feeling to direct it toward your desired result. This is the first step to creating a new reality. Next, focus on what it is you will attract into your life. Focus on the peace you desire for our society. Just as terrorists' intentions are absolute, so can be your desires of peace. Your heartfelt desires have enormous power and are absolute with focus and intention especially when they come from a place of love. So, with all of the respect and love I can muster, I focus on my desire for the elimination of all brutality and killing. I manifest it from a place of love. I envision and expect to see it unfold. Peacefully.

Given the composition of our lower brain, we have been conditioned since prehistoric times to have a reactionary impulse of fight or flight when threatened. Our authentic truth, which is processed by our higher brain, suggests that we create our desired outcomes through thought and manifest our outcomes through continued focus on what we desire. Therefore, when considering resolution to terrorism, police/civilian unrest, and overall perceived injustices of the world, simply begin to focus from within. What are the outcomes you desire? Create those desires from your thoughts. Focus on the desired outcome. Reinforce that desire with the intention of love. ALLOW the events to unfold in the absence of resistance. This allows for creation from the inside out. And always remember...YOU have the power because YOU are made in the image of God.

THINK/WRITE/DO

Three Simple Steps to Creating Your Desired Outcome...

1. **Identify the Problem**—Identify the situation, circumstance, person/people, etc. that you don't like or is making you uncomfortable. Be detailed in exactly what troubles you concerning it. Explore all of your emotions that surround it. We want to expose any and all feelings you have regarding the perceived trouble.

2. **Focus On the Solution**—Focus on what you consider to be the solution to the trouble. Do not focus on the problem. Only focus on the solution. The solution should be based in love, compassion, and understanding for all involved. Allow love, compassion, and understanding to invade your emotions regarding the perceived trouble.

3. **Imagination**—Close your eyes and use the power of your imagination to envision what things look like once your solution has been implemented. Be very detailed with what that looks like but more importantly focus on what that feels like to you. The more you feel it, the stronger the vibrational marker you create.

That is the marker the Universe responds to in delivering your desired result.

By doing these three simple steps, you have put a new reality into motion. You are no longer bound by what you see from the outside world to dictate your internal feelings or present realities. You have become the co-creator God intended you to be. Your new reality may not manifest right away. But what's most important is to continue to be in vibrational resonance with what you truly desire. If you maintain that...it WILL come.

Chapter 42

Mindful Parenting: Consciously Raising Our Children and Ourselves

I recall once having the opportunity to keep my godson while his parents went away on vacation. It was a challenging undertaking to say the least. I had not had a 10-year-old to be responsible for in several years. While he was certainly a delight and joy to be around, he was also a challenge as he demonstrated disruptive behavior at both home and school to the point of his teachers having to contact me several times. This challenged the very thing I'd been trying to practice and implement in my life—patience, a release of judgment, and managing, NOT suppressing, anger. Although we only had a week together, it was very interesting observing the changes my child-rearing had gone through since raising my own son who was soon to be 25 at the time.

In this world of clichés and coin phrases, there's been a lot of talk about mindfulness and being **present** in the moment. We hear about mindful eating, mindful working, "whatever you do, be present and mindful while doing it." This sets the context of this chapter's discussion of mindful parenting and ways we can break the traditional approaches to better managing our children and relationships.

Mindful parenting is moment-to-moment, nonjudgmental attention to a situation or occurrence. It means approaching your child in their behavior or misbehavior from a standpoint of love. Whereas we typically observe a tough situation and react to the behavior, mindful parenting means participating from a place of enlightenment created from the alignment of your inner-self. If you could step outside of that triggered reaction for a moment and observe it (as neutrally as possible), what does it call forth in you to look at, become more aware of, or perhaps to consider an alternative approach or perspective towards your child and the situation? Many times we attempt to make our children prototypes of ourselves. We remove their independence and water down their own guidance system by imparting our desires on them, instead of allowing them to discover and cultivate their own God-given guidance. Mindful parenting means detaching from outcomes and focusing more on what's being presented in a given situation and teaching our children through our own alignment.

For example, as soon as I went to pick up my godson, I was immediately faced with a challenge where he demonstrated behavior and language towards his older sister that I qualified as unacceptable. There was name calling on his behalf and behavior that warranted an immediate solution. When it happened, my initial knee-jerk response was to attempt physical control over the situation. I remembered my previous instinct, which was to chide and punish, with the approach that the more severe the punishment, the more the point got across to my godson. I remembered the feeling of being somewhat out of control when my own children would act out and feeling the need to really "deal" with the situation. So, for this moment, I decided to take a mindful, centered approach to curb that urge and decided to have a heart-to-heart discussion where I did **more listening and less talking**. I used what my godson gave to me to guide the conversation in the direction of teaching. His feelings poured out and I learned more about how he ticked and discovered the things that really mattered to him; his insecurities, his fears, and how he had learned to resolve conflict. But most importantly, I was able to teach him from the clarity of my own example of how there's only one thing in life that you can control and that's YOU! All because I did less talking and more listening. I asked non-judgmental questions. I didn't levy his insecurities against him. I was calm, relaxed, and focused.

I don't believe in forced apologies, however, I did suggest that he think about what he'd said and encouraged him to say something of remorse to his sister. Through the process of alignment with my inner-self, I was able to have an intelligent discussion with a 10-year-old on managing emotions and why/how those emotions and the management of them are most beneficial to him. I didn't judge him on what he said or labeled how he'd behaved as being bad or inappropriate but rather guided him to look at what the outcome of his actions were versus what he desired the outcome to be, and ways he could get a different outcome next time. I know this may sound like higher-level mental processing than what a 10-year-old can handle, but I believe children are much smarter than we give them credit for, and that given more opportunities, they will meet our expectations of them whether the behavior is wanted or unwanted. I purposely chose not to use the adjectives 'good' and 'bad' because those terms are qualified on an individual level. Also, not qualifying the situation or behavior as 'good' or 'bad' allows for more open dialogue and clarity for positive solution.

After the discussion, my godson said to me, "I feel bad that I said that to my sister." I thought to myself, "This is exemplary of him to come to his own conclusions regarding his behavior through our discussion." And that is exactly what we want as parents—for our children to come to their own discoveries and conclusions through the contrast of their own life experience. This was a good lesson in self-awareness and learning how to be conscious of the only real thing you have control over—your response.

What did I learn? I learned that paying attention to my thoughts doesn't mean that we don't have challenging feelings anymore along this journey of alignment and living with intention. Indeed, we may become *more* aware of them. But, with practice and persistence, we are able to let them go more easily. Irritation and anger will pass more quickly. Over time, negative emotions and feelings can pass through so quickly and not even have a significant impact on your experience. You'll be surprised. In addition, I was able to see the positive much sooner in an emotionally charged situation. I used that positivity to assist in remedying the circumstances from a more sound and stable position based on how I envision my inner being would view and handle it—more allowing and forgiving, less resistance and unforgiving. I couldn't stop or control my godson's actions, but I could control where I placed my attention and how I managed my emotions.

It won't always work as you plan. But over time and practice, you'll have more and more wins. We have the ability to choose how we are feeling and reacting to all that is around us at any given moment, allowing us to mold, shape, and create our reality. It's about progress, not perfection. Practice is essential for mindfulness and alignment to work.

THINK/WRITE/DO

Now it's your turn.

- As you're faced with challenges from your children, try taking a different approach towards teaching and discipline when they act out.

- When you're faced with challenges from your spouse, significant other, co-workers, the person who cut you off in traffic, practice mindfulness of the moment and what moment you are choosing to create next.

- How do you keep from exploding at your children yet still impart to them the education of consciousness? Practice your inner alignment. Acknowledge gratitude. Choose happiness. Meditate frequently.

- We are a new generation of parents, determined to make a change, and make peace and well-being a priority, especially through the raising of our children.

Chapter 43

The Eye of the Storm

In 1998, I experienced Hurricane Georges while living in St. Thomas, U.S.V.I. The hurricane was a category 4 with sustained winds of 115 mph. Needless to say, it was very exciting and very scary at the same time. I remember boarding up our apartment, collecting water and stockpiling canned goods in preparation for the storm. Batteries, flashlights, tarp, a radio — all were things we anticipated we'd need post-hurricane. When the hurricane got close, we realized we were not in the safest place, so we went to stay at a very nice hotel where they also had a generator to keep things somewhat operational.

Being this was the first hurricane experience of my life, I knew from the news how to prepare, but I didn't know exactly what to expect. What I saw next was truly awesome in every sense of the word. I remember sitting in the middle of the bed worried about what would happen. Would we be safe? Would we be hurt? Or worse? Would our material possessions be spared or lost?

As the hurricane hit St. Thomas and I sat there in the middle of the bed, I remember my ears popping from the pressure as if I was on a plane. The water in the toilet would suddenly disappear and then come rushing back. The palm trees, thick at their trunks, bent down to the ground with the powers of the wind. The normally calm Caribbean Ocean swelled with 20-foot waves. Roofs, glass, debris all flew through the air. Then there was calm. Absolute calm. Eerie calm. The sun poked through the clouds and all was peaceful. For 30 minutes. Then Hurricane Georges gave us round two of its wrath. The winds picked back up. The rain started again. The roofs, glass, debris, and trees all started to fly away and sway THE OPPOSITE DIRECTION. When all was said and done, Hurricane Georges took 600 souls and did $10 billion in damages from the Lesser Antilles through Haiti, Puerto Rico, Cuba, and the U.S. mainland.

This experience, while devastating to some and less impactful to others, symbolizes our daily lives. The hurricane came through with seemingly reckless abandon. Destruction. Annihilation. Damage. Ruin. These are the winds that attack our daily lives and seek to obliterate happiness, joy, contentment, and peace. We look to "prepare" for the storms by hedging our bets for disappointment, i.e., "Well, I know it won't work out so I'll just be okay staying in the same place if it doesn't work." Or we relegate our circumstances as something elusive or beyond our emotions such as "Well, it is what it is." Or we have developed a sense of unworthiness that keeps us stagnant—"Well, it's just the way my life goes, so I'm just going to go with it." But more specifically, the hurricane winds symbolize seemingly uncontrollable chaos that we tend to accept as real. But the authentic reality is, we control the calm.

As I experienced Hurricane Georges, I realized after it was over that the 30 minutes of peace when I thought the hurricane was complete was actually the eye of the storm passing over the island. The eye of the storm was completely calm yet it was surrounded by destruction, annihilation, damage, ruin, and chaos. The eye of the storm allowed for the sun to peak through and provided a sense of relief, peace, and serenity. It was quiet, tranquil, and still. In our everyday lives, we should strive to **live in the eye and not in the chaos of the winds**. The eye is the inner you. Your authentic being. Your true reality. Discovering the inner, quiet, still being that is your true authentic self provides protection against the destructive, blustering chaos of what we live every day. The anarchy of the world's challenges. The disorder of the judicial system. The turmoil of your working environment. The disarray of unsatisfying and disappointing relationships. Being the eye of the storm or, in other words, living from within, provides the peace, tranquility, and serenity we all covet. Being the eye of the storm, or living from within, provides a safe haven that produces joy, happiness, and peace, no matter the surrounding circumstances.

When the winds of chaos begin to blow, look inward to discover the natural happiness, joy, peace, and love you seek. These gifts are not achieved from receiving from the outside in, but are created from the inside out. Walking and living in the eye of the storm allows us to be confident, happy, loving, and self-assured no matter the outside circumstances because they are just that…outside circumstances. Even when you feel they are happening directly to you, they still remain outside circumstances. You have the power to manifest your calm in the midst of it all. We are not relegated to being victims of our circumstances. Instead, we are empowered to co-create the circumstances we desire. We are endowed to create and manage the emotions we desire most at any given moment in time. We have the ability to produce whatever we want in the current moment and construct something different in the very next moment. Be proactive in your creation, as God has ordained, instead of being a passive observer of your life as it passes you by and delivers what you have simply responded to instead of created. Commune with God, your Creator, in prayer. Find yourself in meditation. Create your physical life from your soul.

Live in the calm. Not in the chaos that surrounds you.

Chapter 44

Knowing What You Really Want

"What this power is, I cannot say. All I know is that it exists…and it becomes available only when you are in the state of mind in which you know exactly what you want…and are fully determined not to quit until you get it." — Alexander Graham Bell, 1847-1922, Inventor and Educator

Do you know what you want? What are your desires? Do you even have any wants or desires? Have you clearly identified them? This may sound simplistic and trivial. Who doesn't know what they want, right? It has been said, in the process of manifestation, knowing what you want is the first step to creation. What does clear vision do? How does knowing what you want, give you power in creating?

When asked the question, "what do you want," most people might say "I just want to be happy" or "I want more money, I want to be financially independent" or perhaps "I want to be in a committed relationship." So, why don't we have these things and why does what we say we want appear elusive and slow to come, if ever? We were put on this earth to create. Period. We were born to manifest greatness! We are all children of the Most High God. We are born with the sole purpose of creating and exemplifying the true power from which we came. We are always wanting and desiring something whether we are conscious of it or not. We are constantly asking for different things verbally and through our vibration. Our wants and desires are fodder for creation. The challenge is, many times, we offer energies that are in direct contradiction to one another and stifle the progress to achieving what we desire. We state from our mouths what it is we want, but our vibration offers something else, something contradictory to our actual desires.

A woman proposed the following statement, "I've been saying I really want to be in a committed relationship, but do I really believe there are good men out there for me? Do I even have the time to devote to being in a committed relationship?" This statement was interesting as her desires seem to be conflicted. This speaks directly to the heart of the concept. Is her energy focused on the desire to be in a committed relationship or is her energy focused on the doubt of finding a "good man" and the time she has devoted to other things? Aligning our energies with our desires is what moves us forward. You see, I don't think many would be hard-pressed when asked to provide an answer to what they want. But often we are conflicted whether we realize it or not.

Many of us, having been caught up in the "Matrix of life" have lost knowing what we want because we are caught up with what is directly in front of us and have labeled it as our authentic reality. (ref: Chapter 2— Escaping the Matrix) However, as it stands, if you don't have what you truly desire, why not? Of course, there are various reasons we come up with. But the truth of the matter is, usually there is something you want MORE than the thing you are expressing verbally. Remember, we are all vibrational, energetic beings and the Law of Attraction is constantly yielding to us exactly what our essence reflects.

For example, the woman previously mentioned, had stated for years that she wanted to be in a loving relationship but found herself involved with men who were either unavailable and/or demonstrated undesirable behaviors. This was because the essence of what she *really* wanted was something else. "I want to be married," but more than wanting to be married, I don't want to sacrifice myself, give up my identity, and lose myself in another individual. Or, "I want a committed relationship," but what I *really* want is to not be hurt anymore and go through the pain of a failed relationship. Or, "I want a loving relationship," but what I *really* want more is to not feel rejected from yet another unfaithful person who desired someone other than me. So, the Universe with its infinite intelligence, and in accordance to the Law of Attraction, kept her safe by co-creating life experiences that gave her what she truly wanted. The Universe does not respond to what you say, the Universe responds to what you **feel;** it responds to the vibration you are emitting, the essence of who you really are. This is why what we say we want and what we receive are different. **We can never have what we are in vibrational resistance to!**

The same can be stated with regards to anything else we say we want. You say you want to be rich and financially independent. But what you really want more is to not feel broke, destitute, or penniless. What you really want is to avoid the pain of disappointment, the pain of trying something independently and failing. So, you never take the perceived risk associated with a new business venture, a new job, or promotion, and you never follow your true passion because at the root of what you truly want is the safety, security, and comfort of what's familiar to you.

When we ask for things from a place of lack, need, not having, missing, fear, or any negative emotion, we get more of the same. The Universe responds to the emotion, to the vibration of our frequency. This is a YES Universe, and it is responding yes to the essence of who we really are. Our lives reflect back to us that which we are! Therefore, when we offer an emotion, and a vibration of expectation and abundance, the Universe responds in kind. It doesn't matter what the current circumstances look like. So, first, understand there is no such thing as lack in an infinite universal space. There is only abundance.

The challenge is to be honest with yourself in *knowing*, on a deeper level, what you want. Identify those deep, hidden secrets that only you and your Creator know. Shine a light on those hidden secrets and expose them in your consciousness. When we take this step, we then remove the resistance, the barrier that has been stagnating our true desires. Now we have the clear vision, the target point of where we're going. From this point, we have clear direction and assurance that we will have what we want.

In the book entitled *The Strangest Secret*, Earl Nightingale draws a parallel between not knowing what you truly want as being like a boat with a sail but without a rudder, sailing aimlessly whichever way the wind blows. The purpose of the rudder is to direct the boat and provide guidance towards the desired destination. The purpose of knowing clearly what you want, which is your vision, is the same, to provide clear direction as to where you're going.

"What this Power is I cannot say..." When we know what we want, power is generated. The power comes from the Inner Source, the God within YOU! Provoking the POWER OF CREATION comes through the process of clearly identifying what you want, isolating and pinpointing your true desires, and having a vision for it all. Whichever religion you have or if you have no religion at all, it doesn't matter. What MATTERS is that you can experience this power.

THINK/WRITE/DO

Going forward, ask yourself some questions:

1. What do I truly want?
2. Why do I want it?
3. Why don't I have it?
4. What am I going to do to achieve it?

Honestly answering these questions will provide clarity, direction, and the empowerment necessary to make more confident decisions, knowing that you now have harnessed a power and force, a divine assistant to help co-create and bring into fruition those things that you want and desire.

Chapter 45

Marry Yourself and Divorce Your Ego

Ego. *"The part of the mind that mediates between the conscious and the unconscious and is responsible for reality testing and a sense of personal identity." —* Webster's Dictionary.

"…reality testing and a sense of personal identity." Inherently this definition is flawed because it suggests that reality is less of a creation and personal identity is measured with outside influence. In authentic truth, we create our own reality and personal identity should be measured from within. However, we all tend to be captive to our egos and we take great time in cultivating it.

As a practical example, outside of protecting one's self, what other need is there to have a physical altercation? So, why do people fight? Because you took my parking space? Because you spoke to me the wrong way? Because you don't agree with my point of view? Therefore, we must by all means "defend" our position. The ego is what says "you must physically pay for taking my parking space." The ego says, "I will not be 'disrespected' by anyone therefore, I must 'defend' my position!" Or, "I will physically harm you because we have differing views." All the while, the extra walk in the parking lot is not life-threatening, the tone of how someone speaks doesn't physically harm us, and God has given every human a point of view and they may differ.

Sometimes, we allow our ego to rule over lives. Ego separates, delineates, and segregates. Ego creates a sense of "reality" that motivates action that has the ability and power to take you out of alignment and into chaos for the sake of ego. Ego is concerned only with itself. Ego has a low self-esteem and is deathly afraid of being exposed. Ego can incarcerate the mind.

We do many things daily that reflect the power our egos have over our lives. Many of us want to be heard, recognized, acknowledged, or praised. There is nothing 'wrong,' in the context of whatever is 'right' or 'wrong,' with wanting to feel those emotions. What should concern us is when we have a **need** to have those feelings to define our self-worth. This is how the ego functions. It functions off the false insecurities it has created and you have allowed to reside in the hallows of your mind.

One of the ways to counter the effects of ego is through enlightenment. Enlightenment is self-awareness. It is unrestricted at the most fundamental level. It is free of judgment. It is open and expectant of all possibilities. It is love. Ego restricts and restrains by constantly having to prove itself worthy of your soul's attention. When not enough attention is given, ego creates fear, doubt, worry, and anxiety, which commands our attention and reassures the ego's existence. So, let us first understand that our egos do not make our authentic being. Our authentic being is free of egotistic control.

I always admire great actors and their art, people like Anthony Hopkins, Sydney Poitier, Robert De Niro, Cicely Tyson, and many more. They become the people they are portraying in their art. But that's not who they truly are. Those are roles they play. Such is the role of ego.

Imagine yourself as a great actor being able to truly immerse yourself in an acting role. You don't have to look very far because this is what we do daily. We play a different "role" every time we leave home and go to our places of employment. We play a different role when we go to social events with our friends. We play another role when we go to church or to the supermarket or to our kids' soccer games. This isn't to say we are not being our true authentic selves, however, we begin to think that the other things around us actually make us who we are. The influences of things, circumstances, and status tend to become the things our egos measure and label as success or failure. We become lost and confused with what is true reality and then our egos begin to define our lives. We start to depend on our ego to define our role in everyday life.

Imagine if Arnold Schwarzenegger thought he was truly The Terminator walking around speaking like a robot and destroying things in the name of saving us all from an apocalyptic world. It's just as ridiculous a notion to think we are defined by the size of our home, the cost of our car, the position at our job, or our status in our community. But the ego keeps us confused. The ego plays as cataracts over the eyes of your soul, distorting your view of authentic truth and reality. Your true authentic being is created in God's image and is empowered to create. This power isn't far off or mythical but operates in the natural order of all things. We must learn not to depend on ego to define our being, but let our being be the authentic truth.

Deepak Chopra said, "The core of my soul is the ultimate reality." The core of your soul is full of peace, harmony, and love. It is who you truly are. It does not put on any fanfare, longing for the attention of others. It is humble and confident within itself. It knows no limitations or boundaries; therefore, it knows nothing of selfishness. It is love. It is you. Know yourself and live in your true existence. Strive to be perpetually aware of your authentic being and your true identity. Life is all about remembering who you are and increasing your awareness. Understanding your BEING allows you to direct and command the ego as opposed to your authentic existence being defined by the ego. Spend intimate time with your authentic self. Don't court your ego when you can be married to the authentic you.

Chapter 46

We Are God's Reality Show

I know. The title alone makes some cringe, right? "What are you talking about? We aren't part of some made up drama by God!" And…we're not. But we create the drama that keeps us in this re-occurring "reality show" of theatrical events full of comedy and tragedy where we play protagonist and are in constant battle with some antagonist, both real and/or perceived. Our lives become one big production that we are hoping will have a happy ending. We make ourselves out to be spectacles. How dissimilar is that to "The Bachelor" or "The Bachelorette?" Or "Big Brother?" Or "Survivor?" Or the funniest of all that is considered one of the pioneering reality shows, "The Real World?"

Ponder the following…

> "Whatever is in the mind is like a city in the clouds. The emergence of this world is no more than thoughts coming into manifestation. From the infinite consciousness, we have created each other in our imagination. As long as there is 'you' and an 'I,' there is no liberation. Dear ones, we are all cosmic consciousness assuming individual form."
> — Vashistha

In Chapter 2, "Escaping the Matrix," we touched on this ideal. The authentic truth is that your soul is living in this world that has been co-created by us. God the Creator is the one who was never born and will never die, the one who created us all in the same image. God's creation continues to perpetuate itself through our thought, desire, and creativity.

So, it stands to reason that all that you see around you is the material expression of another's thought (minus the organic, living things on this earth of course), collectively accepted by us all to create "the reality" we see. In a nutshell, we all have desires. We contemplate those desires, whether that be for more comfort, better health, production efficiencies, families, etc. Our lives are made of desire. Then we put thought to those desires and how to achieve what we desire. Then we act towards the manifestation of what we desire and creation happens. When that creation happens or our desires are manifested, we call that reality.

Here's a factual example: Anthropologists discovered early humans and have identified a number of evolutions in humankind. But let's begin at the Neanderthals. Neanderthals walked the earth some 200,000 years ago, or around the middle Paleolithic era. They used tools and often resorted to using rocks (or flakes broken from rocks by hitting them with other rocks), bones, and sticks. At some point, they even discovered the uses of fire. As time moved forward, the Neanderthals became Cro-Magnons. The Cro-Magnon man used tools, spoke and probably sang, made weapons, lived in huts, wove cloth, wore skins, made jewelry, used burial rituals, made cave paintings, and even came up with a calendar. The changes and differences in these early humans took place over 75,000–100,000 years.

How is it that we went from banging on rocks and grunting to communicate, to using skins for warmth, painting, and singing songs? Because of thought, desire, and creativity. Fast forward to the modern day where we don't hunt or forage for food like a Neanderthal or Cro-Magnon. When we are hungry, we stop at a drive-through and order! We don't use flint to make fire, we flip a switch. We don't kill buffalo for meat and use their skins for warmth, we buy bison in the grocery store and go to the mall to buy a coat if we're cold. Thought, desire, and creativity.

So, whatever you believe in terms of creation, meaning the beginning of time, we are created in God's image, which allows us to continue to evolve through creation. The creation that WE create. We are living in that manifestation. Enlightenment provides an understanding that we are not living in the world, the world is living in US. Most of us have forgotten that authentic truth. THAT is why we are God's reality show.

Dolphins are not gluttonous. Birds don't kill for fun. Whales don't have wars with other pods of whales. Lions don't marry, have cubs, get divorced, and split their assets of the African plains. Animals DO exactly what they were made to do. Every single time. We, as humans, feel we are higher in form because of logic and the "advanced human brain." The fact is, we are the ones who tend to forget our way. Our instinct. Our innate makeup. So, God watches over all of us, all of us in our "highly adapted and intelligent" fortitude and glory, as if we have life figured out. The fact is, we are slaves to our creations. We have forgotten that what we have conceived has been created. We have forgotten that we have the power to continue to create anew.

The only reason that life continues to exist is because of death. But death is not to be misunderstood as finality. Death is rebirth. So in other words, in order to create new, more desirable experiences and fortuitous circumstances in THIS life, death of the old expectations and ill-conceived notions must occur. Past experiences do not determine future outcomes with absolute certainty. If the Neanderthal had never had a thought of an improved life, the Cro-Magnon would have never existed, which means neither would the Homo sapiens (us).

We continue to grow and evolve through creation. But we must focus our vision on what we desire in the moment. The gift we have is the present. This very moment. Not the past. Not the future. The moment. We can create ANYTHING we desire in this moment. To be clear, this does not suggest that we are all some type of witch or magic genie where we make a wish and POOF, what we desire appears. However, by discovering our heart's desires, making our intentions known regarding those desires, and applying our focused attention to those desires, we begin to create the realities we want and wish for.

Understanding this and changing your perspective will focus your authentic reality and help you "see" clearly. Everything that you've seen and experienced thus far can be equated to that "reality show." There is some truth to the events, but there are also some staged, instigated, and false truths to it all. An enlightened perspective will give us clarity in what is real and what is fabricated through our own mental creation. Living from the core of our souls, our authentic selves, provides for truth and precision of what is actually real, shining a light on the façade that has been created and labeled as reality.

Chapter 47

The Anatomy of Anger, the Construct of Bliss

Have you ever contemplated the anatomy of anger? Most of us have not. Where does it begin? How/why is it perpetuated? How do we get rid of it? Or better yet, how do we avoid it? Is it avoidable? We all tend to go along with the flow of emotion as it comes. But what if you could see it from the outside?

So, imagine your emotions as a flowing river. Anger comes down the river like a Cat 5 white water rapid. It's blustery, unruly, and difficult to navigate. But what if you could rise above the river and watch as the anger passes and continues to flow until it dissipates at the river's gulf? Would you do it to avoid all the rough and turbulent water? Or would you continue to ride the river's wave of anger?

Isolating emotion in this way allows us to observe, decide, and then create. Think about the desired emotions you have — joy, happiness, peace, contentment — these emotions are stifled or pushed aside when anger shows up. Think about how your body literally feels when you are angry; your face frowns, your muscles tighten, your jaw grits, your heart rate increases, your breathing is accelerated. You become very tense. You become constricted. Anger immobilizes all other emotions except for the ones that align with it. This is the anatomy of anger. It restricts, inhibits, and stifles any and all desired emotions. Some say, "Well, I WANT to be angry about this!" Or "I have a RIGHT to be angry!" Or perhaps, "Wouldn't YOU be angry if they did that to YOU?!" Well...maybe. But don't use these readily available excuses to retard what you desire to feel.

Justifying your anger does not excuse your responsibility to yourself. In other words, it doesn't matter what the circumstances are/were to make you think that you have a right to be angry. What matters is, what is it that you desire to truly feel?

Buddha said, "Holding onto anger is like drinking poison and expecting the other person to die." The anatomy of anger in the literal sense is also the anatomy of disease. The cells in our bodies operate in synchronicity. They operate harmoniously. One trillion cells in the human body started as one cell that now makes up over 250 different types of cells all operating with specific functions. Anger, frustration, worry, fear…these emotions that make up the anatomy of anger work to restrict the flow of your cells. This is scientific fact. Are you ever exhausted after a big blow up or fight? Are you tired after an argument? Do you fall into a depressive state after being angry for an extended period of time? These are the physiological symptoms of how your emotion has affected your body. High blood pressure, heart attack, stroke can all be brought on starting with anger. Let go of that which does not serve your well-being and begin to construct bliss.

Bliss encompasses joy, happiness, harmony, pleasure, enjoyment, and delight. These should be the coveted emotions we seek. Why? Because operating within bliss also provides a free flow for desires to be cultivated and realized. So, for example, if we use another analogy of a river, negative emotion is like a dam in the river, restricting the current and choking the flow. When bliss is achieved, it all flows naturally and without impediment. Allowing your emotion to flow in bliss opens the flood gates of possibility and the realization of desire. Flowing in bliss offers the Universe the vibrational marker needed that will help you realize your authentic happiness and joy.

Think about a time when you were extremely happy about something. Close your eyes and put yourself back in that place. Allow yourself to relive the emotion that you felt in that moment. Did you feel light? Almost floating? Your outlook on the future was bright. Nothing negative could steal away the joy you felt in that moment. If it tried in that moment, you responded in a much more positive way concerning that intrusion of negativity. We have all experienced this type of feeling, this type of bliss.

We have all experienced the authentic, unimpeded flow of our emotional river. And when it flows, we feel great. We feel free. We feel fantastic. It's that feeling when we're in a "good" mood. Bliss. Now, what if you could feel that on a daily, perpetual basis?

The construct of bliss is not complicated. It is not hard to achieve. You don't need to spend time in a monastery or holy temple for 40 years to realize it. Bliss is readily available to all of us at all times. Bliss is a part of our innate being. It simply waits for us to decide when we will embrace it. There are a few different ways to aid in the construction of the perpetual bliss you desire.

- **Meditate** — Meditation allows you to be in touch with your authentic self, the self that is absolute truth. Be in touch with your soul because your soul is your true self. Spending time inward allows you to better understand and put into context what is outward. It allows you to discern authentic truth.

- **Lose Judgment** — Judgment restricts, stifles, and attempts to control. Every single person experiences this world differently. Even within the same household, workplace, in everyday life...every person's experience is unique to that person. Lose the judgment to free your mind and allow for opportunity to flourish in your life. Judgment jams the river of your emotion the same as anger.

- **Perspective** — Create your perspective. In any given moment, you have a choice to create whatever perspective you desire. This is a powerful proposition. This entire life is made up of individual moments. So instead of worrying about outcomes, focus on the moment you currently are in and mold and shape that moment the way you'd have it to be. As we spoke about in Chapter 3, "Tell Your Thoughts What to Think," when you do this, your perspective will be a slave to your desires.

- **Expectation** — Remember, the Universe will respond to the exact vibrational marker you emit. However and whatever we are thinking, expecting and focusing on, whatever the topic, is what will return to you. Positive OR negative. A combination of both in each situation, nullifies the desire. So, in other words, if you desire and **believe** to have a certain promotion and in the next thought you **believe** you won't be able to get it, then you have successfully confused the Universe and stifled progress. The Law of Attraction is absolute. Guard your expectations and hold yourself accountable to what it is you expect.

- **Envision** — SEE yourself in your desired state and let that first envisioning be your happiness, joy, pleasure, delight, and contentment. Again, these are the emotions that open you to all possibilities of desire and allow them to flow to you. This is your river flowing without impediment. These are the emotions that provide vibrational markers where the Universe responds with more of the same — more bliss. More bliss provides more allowing. More allowing provides more openness for possibilities. More openness for possibilities provides more desires to be realized and delivered to you.

Anger is one of many emotions we feel on a regular basis. It is a very powerful emotion. Love is also a very powerful emotion. Perhaps that's why there is a thin line between the two. However, love is open and free flowing while anger is closed, stifling, and restrictive. Be open. Be open to receive those things that you desire. Finding, practicing, and living in bliss opens your life to infinite possibilities and unlimited joy, happiness, pleasure, and contentment. Bliss is the ultimate exuberance and calm at the same time. Choose to create the happiness you desire. Choose to be happy.

Chapter 48

Turning Thoughts Into Things

We've all heard it, read it, even said it and tried it. How do we take a *thought* and turn it into a *thing*, a true manifestation? How do we bring our desires from the non-physical to the physical? From mental images to real life? Touch it, taste it, see it, smell it, hear it realities?

> *"Everything is energy and that's all there is to it. Match the frequency of the reality you want and you cannot help but get that reality. It can be no other way. This is not philosophy. This is physics." — Bashar*

Turning thoughts to things means taking an idea and turning it into an experience, a result, or a tangible material effect. The truth of the matter is we are always manifesting something! Either purposefully or by default. Either wanted things or unwanted things — *manifestation* happens. The question is, are we manifesting wanted things in our lives or unwanted things? What we want to stress here is that we have the power to start manifesting what's wanted. On purpose. Not by default.

Manifestation—Manifestation is the end result of the process that coincides with The Law of Attraction. However, the Law of Attraction can be a bit misleading for those who are not willing to go through the process. If you truly want to use your energetic/spiritual power to manifest greatness, you must clear all that blocks you from believing in your greatness. You must let go of resistance.

On some level, you've asked for everything that happens in your life. You create your own reality through your intentions or lack thereof. Simply recognizing this one fact can have an enormous impact on your first step towards deliberate creation. Low-level/low-energy thoughts negatively affect your life and high-level/high-energy thoughts positively affect your life. How do you know the difference? Low-energy thoughts feel bad; high-energy thoughts feel good. It's just that simple. You can always tell whether your thoughts have been high- or low-energy by simply looking at what your life is producing and what's going on around you.

Many people, when trying to manifest, focus too much on the outside conditions rather than the internal condition. What's important is our internal experience: whether we *choose* to experience love or fear. When we commit to our internal experience of love, we begin to attract more love. Our progress is impeded and stifled when we approach manifestation from a place of, "How can I get or do something to feel better?" Instead, the focus should be: "How can I feel better FIRST and therefore be an energetic/spiritual match for attracting more greatness into my life?" The emphasis must be placed on the internal condition, not getting a nice new car, promotion, or boy/girlfriend to make us "happy."

Certainly, we have countless evidence all around us, from the Bible to the Quran and many other the religions of the world, where documented accounts show many who mastered the art of manifestation. On the one hand, and as we've discussed in previous chapters, we have come to understand that everything in this material world was once a thought — EVERYTHING! From the vehicle you drive, the residence you live in, the business, career/job you have, even the very way you're reading these words right now (computer or book), it all started first as a thought in somebody's mind. On the other hand, there's that one small ounce of doubt that this is some kind of pie-in-the-sky talk, or that this only works for other people, etc. Even with all this incredible evidence surrounding us, not to mention evidence from our own experiences that we dismiss, we struggle daily with this idea that we have the power to turn our thoughts into things. It feels almost unnatural to believe that the first step to manifestation is not physical action. As a matter of fact, the first several steps are non-physical.

We tend to doubt getting what we want could be this simple. We're taught we must "work hard" (which, to me is code for struggle and stress) to create change in our realities. We've been trained to believe that for our physical realities to change we must do something first — move my body like this, take this class, swallow this pill, get the right job, please the boss, make this top grade in class, jump 100 jumping jacks, eat more veggies, etc. — and then I'll get my result. It's the classic physical cause and effect equation. Its creation by physically doing, trading physical action for physical gains. We have been conditioned to live a goal-oriented life — set the goal, give yourself some target dates, make the goal measurable, and create action steps to take daily towards the goal. While goal setting certainly has its rewards, it is only a very small percentage to actual manifestation, and is last on the continuum of true manifestation — thinking > feeling > THEN acting.

The toughest thing about turning thoughts to things is understanding the importance your emotional awareness plays in the PROCESS of making an idea manifest. We discussed in Chapter 15, "The Eternal Guidance System," the role our emotional guidance plays in our well-being. Our emotions are God's gift to us in navigating through this life with complete joy and happiness. Manifestations become real by **causing an effect**. Thoughts cause effects. Energy causes effects. It's the end results of a thinking, feeling, and acting cycle. Happiness, joy, and love are positive emotions and they are expansive. It's an energy that expands as opposed to "negative" emotions of anger, hate, despair, etc., which are contractive and separate in their effects. Peace movements unite; wars separate.

THINK/WRITE/DO

- The first action step to turning thoughts into things is to simply pay attention (which is an action) to what's happening in your mind while you're going about your day. What emotions correspond to those mental movies?

- Next, focus your thoughts on your desired outcomes, expect your desires to be manifested, and simply believe it to be done. Here's a hint: **You can never out-perform your beliefs.** So it's good to know what your beliefs are.

- Lastly, focus and cultivate the ones that allow for growth of your desires and change the ones that limit and stifle you. Emotion IS the first real manifestation in the process of turning thoughts to things. Is there anything more real than how you FEEL?

Chapter 49

Karma

There is no such thing as coincidence, happenstance, or luck. As I traveled to Las Vegas for work a few years back, I thought about the topic of discussion I wanted to use for our *Align to Enlighten* blog site that week. Karma had been on my mind for a few weeks and I wanted to write about it, but, as it goes in life, sometimes we're unsure of our next steps. Or we second-guess what we should do next. We wrestle sometimes with choice, situation, opportunity, etc. However, when we release and simply **allow**, the Universe provides answers. The answers surround us and are always available to us if we remain in a state of allowance and pay attention to our lives by living in the moment.

So, I was more than pleased when I walked up to a craps table at the Cosmopolitan Hotel and Casino and stood next to a woman on that Thursday afternoon who had a tattoo going down her arm in big letters that read **K-A-R-M-A**. What are "the odds" on that? How much more clarity could the Universe provide? Out of ALL the places and people in Las Vegas, what are the chances that I see THAT woman at THAT time in THAT casino at THAT craps table? A true life example of synchronicity up close and personal. Create clarity — **desire > intention > allow > live in the moment and release the outcome > pay attention.**

Now, let's talk about Karma!

How many times in your life have you heard the saying, "Karma's a bitch?" The harshness of the tone and suggested meaning say that the "wrongs" you've committed in this life are somewhere lurking, just waiting to bring back destruction and ruin to your well-being. It suggests that you are on your way to being judged harshly for your transgressions and there is no hope for your impending demise. But this is misleading to the authentic understanding of karmic cause-and-effect.

Quoting the previous chapter, "Turning Thoughts Into Things," we know: "On some level, you've asked for everything that happens in your life. You create your own reality through your intentions or lack thereof. Simply recognizing this one fact can have an enormous impact on your first step towards deliberate creation." Intention and deliberate creation go hand and hand with karma. Many of us go through life like a leaf floating on a river. We are tossed and turned with the current and rapids of the river. Many simply "go with the flow" of life instead of working and manipulating and directing our flow of life. The leaf on the river has no choice. It goes wherever the water takes it. An enlightened understanding suggests we are one with the leaf and the river at the same time, which allows us to create and direct our journey along the way. It is our **intention** that provides the directive for our karma.

So how do you become a deliberate creator for the karmic pattern of your life? Through your intention. Imagine karma as currency or money. You are the owner of your karmic currency. When you invest in those things that are hurtful or harmful to others, then your dividends are those of destruction and despair. When you invest in the well-being and success of others, then your dividends are paid in the fullness of progress and abundance in your life. Either way, YOU are the deliberate creator of your karmic windfall. When we understand this, we understand that we are no longer the leaf on the river being tossed and turned with no insight as to what happens next. Live in the moment. But pay attention to the moment as you experience the moment and choose actions and thoughts that nurture, uplift, and have good intentions that are born from a place of authenticity to provide the greatest return on your karmic investment.

What about the things I've done in my past? Won't they come back to bite me at some point? That decision is also yours to create. The very first thing to understand about your past and anything from the past you've deemed as "wrong," is to know that there is nothing you can do to change or control the past...OR the future. Again, what you have is the moment. Live in the current moment. So if there are things you've done in the past that you regret and you also feel have karmic repercussions, forgive yourself. Forgive yourself. Forgive yourself. And release it. By releasing it, you are changing the karmic vibration you've created. The more we hold onto regrets from our past and continue to nurture and give them attention, the longer they fester and eventually bring the destruction you are anticipating to your current life. Release it and create a new outcome of expectation.

What about karma for other people? I've been done wrong and I want them to get what's coming to them! First off, wishing bad karma on someone else does not work. Karma is an individual process, not a community process. Secondly, and **most** important, karma functions as a direct ethereal cause-and-effect. So, in other words, wishing for bad karma on someone else ensures that you will have bad karma on yourself. No matter what anyone else has done to you or against you, it is imperative to continue to operate, not from a need to be right in a situation, but simply from a space of desired well-being for **yourself**. So as an example, we don't want to say, "I hope they get what's coming to them!" But more so, "I desire happiness, tranquility, and peace in my life," with no mention or intention of what was done "wrong" to us. Introducing the negative or focusing on the need to be "right" or to "win" mitigates the progressiveness of the positive karma you wish to create for your future. Be selfish with your karma. Your karma is not dependent on anyone else. Remember, receiving the karmic return on investment (ROI) you desire is dependent upon your positive karmic investment in yourself. Focus on the beauty of the whole not the ugliness of the few.

KNOW that you are a powerful creator. At any given moment, which are the only things we control, we have the power to create not only in the present, but also create investments for our future. Make it a habit throughout your day to think positive, nurturing, uplifting thoughts. Let your actions (intent) reflect the same. Focus on your desires while in this state and linger with them. Release the negativity of the past. Negativity of the past means you no good. Let it go and forgive yourself. Allow yourself the freedom to create and be something new. A renewed you. Free to be and create who it is you really want to be. While in this space, again allow your desires to be cultivated. Water them with positive thoughts and provide the sunshine of expectant outcomes, which allows them to grow. Weed out the negativity of doubt and frustration. When your desires don't sprout when YOU think they should or how you think they should, relax and simply release, which will allow them room to grow and flourish. All you really need to do at that point is pay attention. Because at that moment you will see you've created a karmic garden that will yield the flowers of your authentic desires and outcomes. Say to yourself and KNOW, "I am a deliberate and powerful creator." This is the power God has blessed you with. Use it.

THINK/WRITE/DO

Quick Thought…

Karma is not meant to be levied as a form of punishment for all the 'bad' things you've ever done. We create the karma we experience. But it is important that we understand how karma works and take the necessary steps to move our lives forward in the best ways that support our desires. To that end, think about it like this…

> *"Every day that God gives offers each individual a blank canvas upon which to create a masterpiece. Your thoughts and words are your brushes and your paints. Your actions and deeds are the brush strokes you take in creating this masterpiece. Do not allow any of your previous work to influence today's work of art. The past is behind you. If you didn't like yesterday's work, forgive yourself and leave it. Forget about it. Stop giving it the energy today's masterpiece requires. Be in the present. Be in the now. Simply be."* – Align to Enlighten

Chapter 50

The Caterpillar and The Butterfly

"When she transformed into a butterfly, the caterpillars spoke not of her beauty, but of her weirdness. They wanted her to change back into what she always had been. But she had wings." — Dean Jackson.

Eric Carle published a children's book in 1969 called *The Very Hungry Caterpillar*. I'm sure most of us remember reading the caterpillar book as children. I remember the caterpillar ate and ate and ate, fattening itself until there came the day that it spun its cocoon out of silk and eventually emerged as a beautiful butterfly.

Out of the innumerable creations God has put into motion, it still blows my mind regarding the transformation that takes place between caterpillars and butterflies. It is truly amazing because the caterpillar literally transforms into something completely different than what it perhaps THOUGHT was its purpose and destiny. It eats leaves as a caterpillar but drinks nectar as a butterfly. It crawls as a caterpillar but sprouts wings and flies as a butterfly. It lumbers along on feet as a clumsy caterpillar but hovers, jaunts, and floats elegantly on the winds as a butterfly. Are there not similarities of alignment to the enlightenment of your soul?

The caterpillar is not concerned about its ultimate outcome but more about the current moment. The caterpillar operates in its authentic nature thus allowing it to be transformed when the time is right. We, too, are one of God's illustrious creations. We too have a purpose that should be fulfilled. But we tend to be content to remain the caterpillar, which stifles our growth and retards our transformation. We tend to be afraid to transform. Afraid of change. Afraid to fly. "What will others think?" Or, "I'm set in my ways." Or perhaps, "I don't need to change anything! This is just who I AM!" We remain the caterpillar, crawling along through life never soaring to our higher calling. Our higher sense of self. Our higher purpose.

When we stifle our desires to grow, we decide to remain the caterpillar for life. The caterpillar does not have a choice as to what happens next in its life because God has given him the innate ability to transform and the caterpillar simply succumbs to that will that is authentic to itself. As humans, we resist against the will of our authenticity, which in turn stifles our transformation.

We ALL come to this Earth with purpose. However, reason and sometimes faulty logic imprison our fundamental desires, which derail our purpose. If the caterpillar had logic and could speak, it would probably have a similar reaction as a human, meaning, if one caterpillar said to the other, "Man, I want to stop crawling around on these tree branches eating leaves. I want to start flying around here drinking nectar from the flowers instead," the caterpillar's friend would probably respond like we do: "Man, you can't fly! I been in this tree, eating leaves all my life! **You** must be CRAZY thinking that we can fly!"

Is this dissimilar to how we react and respond to the desires we have within us? The caterpillar, whether he realizes it or not, has a much larger purpose than simply being a caterpillar for the rest of its life. As do we. But some, who know what their purpose is, tend to lose sight of what their purposes are. Or we choose not to explore what our purpose might be and fall into the everyday rat race and call it "normal." Or we simply are afraid to explore anything outside of our everyday lives, succumbing to the fear of change. Or sometimes it's the simple fear of disappointment. "What if I go for it, but I fail? Just forget it, I'll just stay right here where it's 'safer' for me." **Finding your purpose will not bring detriment to your life.** Finding and living within your purpose will bring **fulfillment** and **joy** and **happiness** and **contentment** and **abundance** and **peace** and every other satisfied emotion God has blessed us with. In fact, the emotions just listed act as a barometer to your alignment with your purpose. Therefore, it's worth taking stock of your emotional inventory to assess your alignment or misalignment with your current purpose in life.

Finding Purpose in Life

But how do we find our purposes in life? Start with your fundamental desire. Our innate, authentic purpose begins with our desires. We are made up of our desires, which direct us to our purpose (and please go deeper than the desires for those new shoes you want or that exotic sports car you covet). Many times, we think that achieving our desires are just short of the miraculous. But if we stop to look around at God's creation, miracles happen daily. Why? Because everything within nature, except for human beings, operate on natural instinct. This is why a caterpillar can never stifle its purpose to become a butterfly.

Your thoughts and dreams already have a built-in safe and guarded refuge, which is your mind. Yet, we often scold, chastise, denounce, and embarrass our thoughts for simply being thought of as if the entire world is watching. We think about *What If* (Chapter 34) and quickly douse the spark of possibility with doubt and anxiety. Why? Open your mind to the complete catalogue of possibility! **What can be conceived can be created.** Your mind is as fertile as God's Earth. Your thoughts are seeds. The seeds you plant will sprout, grow, and yield the crop you have cultivated. It's as simple as that. When we fail to nurture our seeds with thoughts of positivity and unbounded possibility, our crop becomes stunted and sometimes diseased and ultimately dies on the vine or even before it grows.

THINK/WRITE/DO

Choose first to focus on your fundamental desires. What are you passionate about? What makes you feel content? What makes you happy? Then align those thoughts with unbounded possibilities and a belief that you too have the ability to enjoy life in that abundance—*My fundamental desires are this and that. They make me feel happy and content. I open myself to the possibilities of living within that life.*

Finally, focus your energy, thoughts, expectations, and faith towards those things—*I envision myself living my life within those things and being prosperous in those things.* Close your eyes and take note of how you feel from doing this exercise. Embrace it. See it. Believe it. Rejoice in it because you've found your purpose at this point. Now all you need to do is break your cocoon, which is the monotony of everyday life, and spread your wings to fly in the authentic purpose of your being. Fly.

Chapter 51

I Am

Who do you desire to be in this life? Not the desire of being a successful doctor or some prominent attorney or some real estate mogul. But what type of person do you desire to be? Influential? Charismatic? Friendly? Confident? Loving? Who is it that you desire yourself to be? Are you already that person you desire to be? Perfect in every way? If you're a human like the rest of us, I'm sure there are aspects about your character or person where you desire some improvements. You might desire improvements that could enhance certain relationships; enhancements that may promote a more confident you; enhancements that would serve to bring you more joy in your day-to-day life, etc. But how do we obtain these enhancements?

I know I've tried telling myself that I would be more cognizant of the unwanted behavior I'm displaying in order to try to change myself to a more desired behavior. Sometimes that works while other times I've failed miserably. I remember wrestling for years with my lack of patience. Sometimes I had it under control and other times I did not. I remember having a bad temper and it being my "controller" of my behavior instead of me being the controller of it. We all, invariably, have certain things about ourselves that we perhaps would like to see changed for the positive. But not the yo-yo change of "you've got it working today but can't control it tomorrow." Or the yo-yo change that is dependent upon the situation. Like, I'll have patience with Bob but never with Mary. The first part of understanding the peace we seek in sustained change and growth is to understand we have the ability to effect change simply by focusing our desires. In this chapter, we will discuss how to create and live with sustained change.

Aham Brahmasmi (ah-HUM brah-MAHS-mee). These words may seem strange and hard to pronounce, but they carry a strong meaning. This is an ancient Sanskrit mantra that means "the core of my being is the ultimate reality." This is true because at the core of your being is your soul. It is your soul that communes with God, our Ultimate Creator. There is only authenticity and truth in this space. All of your soul-felt desires are born in this space. The desire to be a loving mother, a faithful husband, having a charitable heart, the desire to spread love…all are born in the spirit. In searching your soul, you find the ultimate reality, your ultimate desire of who it is you truly desire to be.

Aham Brahmasmi is a mantra designed to bring your soul back into remembrance of what is authentic reality. A mantra is defined as, "a word or sound repeated to aid concentration in meditation. More specifically, a mantra can be seen as a reminder or an affirmation that aids in the achievement of your desires," (Webster's Dictionary), as long as your desires are authentic and not superficial. For example, I may want a new car and I could affirm daily that I drive a Ferrari (superficial), or I may want a new car and I could affirm daily that "I desire and affirm reliable transportation" (authentic). But beyond the "things" we desire, what lies at the core root of who we are and what we desire as human beings as it relates to humanity?

I had dinner with a friend who expressed to me some challenges he was having with his teenage son. (Not at all uncommon, right?) The challenge was the dad was looking to maintain his authority without alienating his son. This is MUCH easier said than done when parenting a teenager. My friend mentioned that his son seemingly didn't care about things the father felt important, such as accountability for his actions. This, of course, led to several blow-ups between the two as the dad was trying to teach life lessons of responsibility to an unwilling student. So, I asked my friend what he desired to happen in this situation with his son. He told me that his desire was to have a healthy relationship with his son that was free of anger, frustration, turmoil, and angst. But some would say that living in a house with a teenager with the expectation of not having anger, frustration, turmoil, or angst is the stuff made of syrupy Hollywood sitcoms like "My Three Sons," "Leave It To Beaver," or "The Cosby Show." But just as Aham Brahmasmi is an ancient Sanskrit mantra still used today by millions to remind us of how to be in touch with authentic reality, we also can create our very own mantras that keep us in remembrance of WHO we are and WHO we desire to be. I will show you how we do this.

STEP ONE:

I used my friend and his son as just one example. But for your life, make a short list of character traits you wish to be more prevalent and prominent in your behavior. For example, you may want more patience because you know that it will serve you well with your relationships on your job or in your home. You may want to express more love, compassion, joy, happiness, confidence, leadership, humility, tranquility, calm, peace... any number of positive character traits you desire for your life. Write them down. Be sure you take some time to seriously think about what traits you desire most and be true to YOURSELF because this is an exercise for you and only you. Doing this exercise will indirectly affect others around you, but the primary goal is not to affect change in them, but in YOU. What are the positive traits you desire more of in your life? Take some time to write them down now.

STEP TWO:

Once you have your list written out, and it doesn't have to be expansive, you're NOT that "messed" up, place the words "I Am" in front of each of the positive traits you desire for yourself. So, I Am...patient. I Am...peace. I Am...a leader. I Am...love. I Am...happiness. I Am...understanding. I Am...tranquil. I Am...a great mother to my children. I Am...humble in my walk. I Am...the moment I create. I Am...in touch with my soul, my authentic self. I Am...in lock-step with my Creator. Build your mantra and affirmations to align with the desires you have for yourself. Again, this is specific to YOU and YOUR behavior and how you want to live YOUR life. It does not matter how others will respond, although you will receive positive feedback simply because you are creating very strong, very positive vibrational markers by aligning with your authentic desires born from your soul. As stated in previous chapters, the Universe responds in kind to the vibrational markers we emit. Therefore, your positivity begets more positivity.

STEP THREE:

This is the most important step of this exercise. Once you have identified your desired positive traits and built your mantra and affirmations, as you begin to recite them to yourself, it is most important to take time with each one of them as you read them and FEEL what it is you are reciting. So if you say, I Am…peace, then take the time before you go to the next one to FEEL what peace feels like. I Am…happiness, then FEEL what happiness feels like in that moment. I Am…the moment I create, then KNOW you have the power to turn around any given moment to make it positive in your life. You ACTIVATE or MANIFEST your mantras, affirmations, and desires by FEELING them and envisioning yourself in operation with them. THIS is the power of co-creation that God has given us. Don't rush through them. Spend time, hesitate and linger in each of your affirmations.

Wake up in the morning and recite your personal mantra and affirmations before you go to work. Visit them throughout your day. Read and feel them again at night. Personally, after "slaying dragons" all day, I make sure I recite my mantras and affirmations once again before I step foot in my house. It simply centers me and puts me back into the authentic place of my soul…Aham Brahmasmi…the core of my being is the ultimate reality.

Chapter 52

═══════════════════════════════════════

The Sweetness of Living This Life

Oh, what a difference a year can make, or month, or a day, or even one hour, or one single moment. You began this journey 51 chapters ago with us. It began with a few simple thoughts of what is authentically real in this life. The journey took us through a better understanding of our perceptions and purpose in life. Then we traveled through chapters regarding energy and emotions, and how our energy and emotions direct our lives and help shape our realities. Then we moved into alignment and what that means. We discussed alignment as the rudder of our life's sailboat providing direction. We finished by discussing enlightenment with the understanding that enlightenment simply means living in full awareness and authentic reality.

As we prepare to conclude for now, we would like to leave you with some highlights of points that we feel will be valuable and helpful to you along your continued journey. Here's what we would like you to remember from Align to Enlighten:

Belief—First, know that your belief shapes every aspect of your life, and that sometimes we have limiting beliefs that unconsciously impede our ability to move forward in achieving our desires. But this isn't what's most important. What's most important is, **you can change your beliefs on any particular subject matter you wish.** Just because you've believed something all your life doesn't mean you must keep believing it. If it no longer resonates with who and what you are TODAY, change it! Ask yourself, what do I believe about this? Is this belief helping or hindering me? If your current belief does not serve you best, meaning if it is not yielding you your ultimate desires, change your belief and know that it's okay. We are all evolving beings, expanding in knowledge through our own life's experiences.

Law of Attraction—That which is like unto itself is drawn. You attract to yourself that which you are. You get what you predominantly think about, whether wanted or unwanted. Your fears, anxieties, frustrations, suspicions, etc. become real based on this law. If you want more of something, think about it, talk about it, and imagine more of it. Capture the emotion of what it feels like to have that which you desire. This creates the platform from which you will receive all that comes to you. God and the Universe are responding to you always! What are you responding to?

Energy/vibration—We are all walking energy fields. This isn't all that we are, but at the core, we are energy and vibratory beings emitting frequencies 24 hours a day, 7 days a week, 365 days a year. Even when we're sleeping. Why is this important to know? Because this frequency is being matched with other frequencies like it. The Universe is responding to us based on our frequency, which basically means our mood, our attitude, how we're feeling at any given point in time. The Universe does not respond to our words, it responds to the essence of how we truly feel, which makes it critically important that we pay close attention to the way we feel and make how we feel a priority ALWAYS! Decide you're going to be happy no matter what. Decide you're going to be joyous no matter what is occurring in life. Watch that joy be delivered back to you.

We create our own reality—Your life experience, your reality that you are presently living, is a depiction of exactly what you have believed, thought about, talked about, and projected feelings and emotions about up to this point. This Universe reflects back to you. It mirrors what and who you are. Remember, thoughts become things. If you're not pleased with the life you're currently living, create a new one. How? By first believing that you can. Second, deciding that you will. Third, decide what kind of life you want for yourself. Then get into the allowing mode to receive new experiences, people, circumstances, and events to take place. **And remember, what is presently happening in your life today doesn't**

mean anything at all about your life tomorrow besides what YOU believe and decide it to mean. There is no relationship between your today and your tomorrow besides YOU. You are the only for sure variable that has any impact whatsoever regarding your life.

Alignment—This TRUMPS EVERYTHING! Do everything within your power to get in and stay in alignment. Alignment with your inner being is one of the most influential things that impacts life. Being in alignment with your inner being on any subject matter that you experience gives you the upper hand on life's circumstances when they occur. Whenever you have an experience, first, know that you created it. You cannot have an experience that you are not a vibrational match to in some shape, form, or fashion. But also, ask yourself how is my inner being looking at this thing I'm experiencing? Your emotions are the key. If you're feeling negative emotion, know for certain that you are out of alignment with your inner being. Do whatever you need to do to get in alignment — deep breathing, meditation, hold a baby, pet an animal, go dancing, walk, run, take a nap, whatever you need to do to release the resistance.

Unconditional Love—Choose love despite the condition. Not loving something that's harmful to you, but rather choosing the **emotion** of love regardless. So your lover has mistreated you —*love regardless*. You lost your job — *love regardless*. Someone is trying to hurt you — *love regardless*. We didn't say love them regardless, although that would serve you very well. We're saying stay in alignment and in harmony with the God force of love. This will empower you beyond measure! Learn to love despite condition. Learn not to depend on a condition to demonstrate love. Don't look for ideal circumstances to love, **just be love!** It's easy to love what's lovable. But true expansion, growth, and power comes from loving when everything around you says, "don't love."

Enlightenment—Understand that enlightenment is not some destination in life. Enlightenment is about being aware. Aware of what? Aware of what is authentic reality in this life. How do we find authentic reality in this life? By being in touch with our authentic being — our soul. How do we do that? We can start with meditation. Communing with the core of your being.

"True consciousness lies in the gap between thoughts." — *Deepak Chopra*

Walking in enlightenment helps us put the world and everything that happens within this world into context. When we can put anything into context, it allows for clarity. With clarity, we are enlightened.

As we embark on a new journey just know that you may not get it all right. You may not get it all done. You may go backwards, sideways, and diagonal just to go straight. But also know you can't really get anything wrong. It all happens for reasons. Just make more decisions on what you prefer in this life. Know that well-being is your natural state. Anything other than that is out of alignment with who you really are. Spend more time doing things you enjoy, things that make you laugh, and things that inspire you. **Realize that we're all in this life together!** We're all striving for pretty much the same things—peace, good health, joy, happiness, prosperity, etc.—and we're here for a very short time, so make the best out of the life YOU want for yourself.

Reflections

In January 2015, Gene Black and Edward Muhammad decided to set out on a quest to share knowledge and information regarding alignment of your soul and enlightenment of your consciousness. Their intentions were to help others by posting one blog per week on Sundays for 52 weeks. We must say we are **more than grateful** that you have also shared this journey with us through the reading of this book.

As we set out with the intention of helping others, *we* were the ones who were most helped. *We* were the ones who were affected in growth and transformation while experiencing an awakening to our true authentic selves. It was this same growth and transformation that fueled us to continue to write and share, in an effort to help others grow spiritually and help to continue to enlighten others for spiritual empowerment. God has given us so much, and we don't mean materially, but ethereally. He has given us the power of our conscious minds, which are designed to manifest and create realities we desire. We are empowered by God to affect change in positive ways. **We can have the peace we desire in this world by simply walking in and manifesting peace in our own daily lives.**

God has also given us tools to further our empowerment. The Law of Attraction is one of those tools we've spoken about. Today, what we call "going viral" and speaking about it as a new term, is simply a reflection of what has always been. The Law of Attraction was the FIRST catalyst for "going viral." **When there are groups of people all generating a similar vibrational marker, the Law of Attraction is designed to make that feeling "go viral."** What we focus on expands. That expansion is compounded when people are all operating in like-mindedness, positive OR negative. At Align to Enlighten, we choose to promote positivity.

We set out in January 2015 to share in the higher consciousness of life here on Earth. Our intentions were to discuss spiritual empowerment along with ways to affect positive change in people's lives while operating from a space of peace, love, and tranquility. Our desires have been, and continue to be, structured around the enlightenment of others while generating very powerful vibrational markers with the sole objective of making peace, love, joy, happiness, and the spontaneous fulfillment of desire **go viral** in a Universal type of way.

We certainly hope and expect that *From Alignment to Enlightenment* has touched you in some type of positive way. We will continue to share, post, discuss, write about, and expand this positivity now and beyond, until peace is the norm, love is common nature, joy is abundant, and success is realized. We desire peace, love, and tranquility for you along your journey. Namaste.

About The Authors

We are first cousins (Edward and Gene) who were raised together a great portion of our childhood like brothers. We come from a tightly knit family with strong, hard-working, faithful parents and grandparents. We grew up members of the Christian Church where we spent a great majority of our childhood. We both agree this was our introduction to spiritual growth and religion. We practically lived at church growing up and our roots remain in that sanctity. Church was more less the catalyst for our spiritual foundation. We learned a great deal about God, Jesus Christ, the disciples, how to live "right" and many other beliefs. Church guided our lives and principles as we grew up. But it wasn't until adulthood that we realized that **spirituality** transcends church.

Our lives took different courses as we both grew older.

Edward: I am the proud product of a single parent (mother) home, who spent every other weekend with my father, sister, step brothers, and step mother. I received home stability at my father's house and the diversity of moving around a lot with my mother. However, although I had stability when visiting my father, it still came at a price because of the environment that surrounded it. I became engulfed in the street life and was eventually incarcerated for a felony crime. I persevered that storm, and eventually married, divorced, and raised two beautiful children. Now I am an entrepreneur, Occupational Therapist, and Empowerment Coach.

Gene: At 12 yrs. old I moved to Flint, Michigan with my mother, sister and stepfather. Flint had and still has its fair share of tests, trials and challenges. But Flint taught me how to survive. Literally. I set my sights on Morehouse College, graduated and moved to St. Thomas briefly before eventually getting married. I now have a beautiful wife and four wonderful children. Since St. Thomas I've made a career in Corporate America for almost 20 years and currently reside in Southern California where I also speak professionally and facilitate online teaching at University of California.

Of course, both our journeys have taken many twists and turns along the way which have helped shape us into the men we are today.

THE TURNING POINT —

There was a turning point that took place with both of us. You know, the point where you know your life will never be the same. The place where you become aware of things like never before. What we understand now is that many of us live a life of inner conflict and outward contradiction. We see ourselves as who we are when we look in the mirror. And that's the person many of us relate to along with our ego and our perceived realities. **But the authentic truth is, we are souls having a human experience. Not humans who experience spirituality from time to time.** The authentic you, the authentic me is the soul that lives within.

It was this point of understanding when we connected beyond any level we had ever connected before throughout our entire lives as cousins. We became conscious of Universal laws and principles and we communicated on these principles daily.

We saw IMMEDIATE changes in each other. We watched one another expand and grow consciously. We watched each other demonstrate tremendous strength in the face of adversity with a new found understanding of spiritual empowerment. We shared our new quest with whomever would listen, and even with those who wouldn't listen. Our conservations suddenly, and seemingly overnight, elevated and transcended into something neither one of us anticipated.

A BLOG IS BORN —

From our respective journeys through this life, and our desire to elevate and improve our own personal lives' circumstances, we decided to create a blogsite on the first Sunday of 2015. **Align to Enlighten** was born. It was created as a platform for us to discuss spiritual growth, spiritual empowerment, self-mastery and to help provide a roadmap for discovering individual inspirational methods and techniques that we both benefit from while helping others realize the same benefits. We formalized and published things we had been discussing and talking about for years. It's funny...now days we can barely even remember what we talked about before we started this mission. Seems like this has been what we've always discussed.

THE VISION —

Our intention and true desire is to inspire. For all those who interact with **Align to Enlighten**, we want you to live an authentically **inspired** life. We want to provoke thought, promote dialogue, and inspire change. There is a paradigm shift taking place. Have you noticed? The collective consciousness of society is shifting. We want to continue to encourage that shift to affect positive change. That shift to a greater understanding of spirituality and manifestation of desire. Those who desire to make the shift of aligning your soul to enlighten your life...welcome.

This is not about religion per se. If you are religious or if you are not religious, Align to Enlighten is created and designed to enhance your spiritual understanding. Align to Enlighten will compliment your spiritual belief and augment your spiritual knowledge. Therefore, if the views shared or expressed here are offensive to you, please note, that it is not our intention. OUR intention, our vision is to share our experiences and understandings of Universal laws and principles that promote self-mastery of ways to live a richer, more fulfilled, and inspired life. After all, the authentic you, is the soul that lives within. The authentic you, communes with God, The Creator, Jehovah, Allah, The Most High, etc. And we are made in HIS image...that image being ethereal...not material. So, the TRUE you and the TRUE me is the spirit within. And spending time with the authentic you, helps provide context to our current and future realities. The realities we choose to create.

ALIGNMENT is what we do to maintain that constant state of being in touch with our authentic selves. And ENLIGHTENMENT is simply about being constantly aware that this context even exists in the first place. Join us on this journey of **Align to Enlighten** to gain a perspective of improving your life through spiritual empowerment.

EDITOR

Monica Dennis, Founder
On-Call Editing
http://www.oncalleditingservices.com/
email: monicaoncall@oncalleditingservices.com
Twitter & Instagram: @monicaoncall
Facebook: On-Call Editing

ILLUSTRATOR

Melissa Morgan
melissamorgancommunications@gmail.com

Melissa's Thoughts About the Book Cover Design:

"The Enlightened One" is a digitized multimedia portrayal of the radiance, balance and peace of an aligned being connected to the circular flow of life energy." Created by Melissa Morgan

9 781524 695040